RIGHT OF MALACHI

:: NORMAN HUBBARD

RIGHT OF MALACHI

EXPLORING THE GREAT IDEAS OF THE NEW TESTAMENT ::

NAVPRESS®

BRINGING TRUTH TO LIFE

OUR GUARANTEE TO YOU

We believe so strongly in the message of our books that we are making this quality guarantee to you. If for any reason you are disappointed with the content of this book, return the title page to us with your name and address and we will refund to you the list price of the book. To help us serve you better, please briefly describe why you were disappointed. Mail your refund request to: NavPress, P.O. Box 35002, Colorado Springs, CO 80935.

The Navigators is an international Christian organization. Our mission is to advance the gospel of Jesus and His kingdom into the nations through spiritual generations of laborers living and discipling among the lost. We see a vital movement of the gospel, fueled by prevailing prayer, flowing freely through relational networks and out into the nations where workers for the kingdom are next door to everywhere.

NavPress is the publishing ministry of The Navigators. The mission of NavPress is to reach, disciple, and equip people to know Christ and make Him known by publishing life-related materials that are biblically rooted and culturally relevant. Our vision is to stimulate spiritual transformation through every product we publish.

Cover design by studiogearbox.com
Cover illustration MedioImages/Corbis
Creative Team: Nicci Hubert, Keith Wall, Debbie Weaver, Darla Hightower, Arvid Wallen,
    Pat Reinheimer

Unless otherwise identified, all Scripture quotations in this publication are taken from the *New American Standard Bible®*, Copyright © 1960, 1962, 1963, 1968, 1971, 1972, 1973, 1975, 1977, 1995 by The Lockman Foundation. Used by permission. Other versions used include: *The Holy Bible, English Standard Version* (ESV), adapted from the *Revised Standard Version* of the Bible, copyright Division of Christian Education of the National Council of the Churches of Christ in the U.S.A. All rights reserved; Scripture taken from the *HOLY BIBLE, NEW INTERNATIONAL VERSION®*. Copyright © 1973, 1978, 1984 International Bible Society. Used by permission of Zondervan. All rights reserved; Scripture taken from *The Message*, Copyright © 1993, 1994, 1995, 1996, 2000, 2001, 2002. Used by permission of NavPress Publishing Group.

Printed in the United States of America

1 2 3 4 5 6 7 8 / 11 10 09 08 07

FOR A FREE CATALOG OF NAVPRESS BOOKS & BIBLE STUDIES,
CALL 1-800-366-7788 (USA) OR 1-800-839-4769 (CANADA).

To Vic Black,

who held the Bible in one hand

and my heart in the other.

For you have been born again not of seed which is perishable but imperishable, that is, through the living and enduring word of God.

For, "ALL FLESH IS LIKE GRASS,

AND ALL ITS GLORY LIKE THE FLOWER OF GRASS.

THE GRASS WITHERS,

AND THE FLOWER FALLS OFF,

BUT THE WORD OF

THE LORD ENDURES FOREVER."

And this is the word which was preached to you.

1 Peter 1:23-25

CONTENTS

INTRODUCTION

THE JOURNEY AHEAD ::

When George Mallory was dogged by reporters in New York to explain why he wanted to climb Mount Everest, he ultimately responded, "Because it is there." For a mountain climber, the simple presence of a mountain makes scaling it the only sensible alternative.

Why should a Christian read the Bible? Because it is there. Not simply because we ought to — but because God wrote a book. Because He is an Author. Because the Creator of heaven and earth wants to communicate with us. What could comprise more inspiring and intimate worship than studying the Scriptures God saw fit to send us?

Many of us, however, find it easy to defer to others in this aspect of Christian worship. We regularly listen to pastors who have studied and prepared messages. We take Christian education classes where lay leaders spell out the precepts they have learned. And we buy books that distill the doctrines down into memorable chapters that tell us how we can walk with God.

All of this is well and good. Hasn't God given "some as apostles, and some as prophets, and some as evangelists, and some as pastors and teachers, for the equipping of the saints for the work of service, to the building up of the body of Christ" (Ephesians 4:11-12)? We ought to take advantage of the best teaching God has provided for His church.

However, none of us is justified in wholly handing off this aspect of our worship to others. We wouldn't dream of doing this with our money or our prayers. All of us are called to give according to our means and to pray according to our faith. In the same way, we are all called to read and meditate on the Bible's message according to our ability.

The example of the Jews in Berea should give us encouragement. When Paul passed their way, preaching that Jesus was the Messiah, these synagogue-goers "received the word with great eagerness, examining the Scriptures daily to see whether these things were so" (Acts 17:11). Our churches should be filled with men and women as noble as those Bereans.

Yet many of us find ourselves bouncing along through life with a Bible on our laps not quite sure how it all fits together and not committed to improving our lot. We know the general sketch of the gospel, but stitching and glue is the only thing that joins much of the Bible together for us.

I am reminded of a Bible study I led several years ago where I asked a group of college men to open up to the book of Habakkuk. Someone in the study looked up at me, smiled knowingly, and said, "That's a good one, Norm. There's no such book in the Bible." He was humbled to discover that Habakkuk is an actual, if little known, book among the Old Testament Minor Prophets.

For this Christian, as for many of us, we have hardly a clue where Habakkuk resides in our Bibles, much less what message binds this prophecy to the rest of the Bible. How are we to make sense of the whole? We are like the Ethiopian official who was riding away from Jerusalem with a scroll of Isaiah spread across his lap. "Do you understand what you are reading?" Philip asked him. "Well, how could I, unless someone guides me?" the man replied (Acts 8:30-31).

Consider this book in your hand a guide to the great ideas of the New Testament. *Right of Malachi* will help you bind together the great themes of the gospel as they are introduced in the Old Testament and fulfilled in the New Testament. Jesus Himself told us, "If you continue in My word, then you are truly disciples of Mine; and you will know the truth, and the truth will make you free" (John 8:31-32). For those who want to walk the path of discipleship with Jesus, the path of freedom in life and into eternity, this guide will help to chart a course.

And if anyone should wonder why you have decided to study the Bible for yourself, a simple answer might suffice: Because it is there.

Enjoy the journey.

A FIRM FOUNDATION

GOD IS THE CREATOR AND SUSTAINER OF OUR WORLD ::

If you're acquainted with the teachings of Jesus or His apostles, you can probably tally up on one hand the number of times you recall any of them talking about the creation of the world. (If you're not familiar with their teachings, even one hand would be unnecessary.)

The New Testament gives no record that Jesus or His apostles ever wrote or spoke at length about how the world was created. This might lead you to wonder, then, if Creation is one of the great ideas of the New Testament.

To answer that question, consider the sitar . . . yes, the sitar. This is a traditional Indian instrument made up of a resonating body (usually a hollow gourd) and a long, fretted neck with seventeen strings. If you've ever played the guitar, you might marvel at the fact that anyone could fret seventeen strings on the neck of any instrument. As a matter of fact, no one does.

Not every string on the sitar is pressed against a fret. Several of them serve as "drone strings," which help to sustain the harmonic tone of a song. While a sitar player frets individual notes on some of the strings, he plucks the drone strings to maintain the tonic texture of a piece. In this way, complex modes of expression can be worked out over a broad interval of individual notes, while the drone strings preserve the background.

If you haven't heard what this sounds like, pick up a CD by Ravi Shankar, the most renowned modern sitar player. (It's reported that he once received a standing ovation after tuning his instrument!) You'll be much the richer for experiencing a portion of world music at its best, and you'll have a door of imaginative access into the theme of Creation in the New Testament.

So what's the relationship between the sitar and New Testament writings about Creation? The idea of Creation doesn't leap onto the stage of New Testament discourse like a raging guitar solo from your favorite rock band. Instead, it resonates in the background like a melodic tone established long before anyone struck up the score of the New Testament.

Jesus stressed the fact that He had not come onto the stage of humankind to abolish the Old Testament but to fulfill it. Indeed, the Old Testament was not "old" to Him at all. When Jesus said things like "the Scriptures . . . testify about Me" (John 5:39), and "the Scripture cannot be broken" (10:35), He was referring to the only Scriptures anyone possessed at the time—what we now call the Old Testament. By His specific teachings and implicit commitments, Jesus affirmed the relevance and authority of the Old Testament.

It is no wonder, then, that the notion of divine creation and a Sovereign Creator grounded all New Testament thinking about God's authority in the world and the creatures' relationship to their Creator.

In the New Testament, we gain an appreciation for the role that nature plays in testifying to God and the role that Jesus plays in sustaining creation. More than all else, we are led to consider the foundations of our faith—that God "is not far from each one of us; for in Him we live and move and exist" (Acts 17:27-28).

A GUIDED EXPEDITION

Introducing the Unknown God. Not until the apostle Paul reached the city of Athens does the New Testament offer any report of a sermon preached to a predominantly Gentile audience. In Acts 17:22-34, Paul identified a common belief that pagan Athenians shared with Christians, namely, that we are obligated to worship the Deity (or deities) who controls our destinies.

1. How did Paul discover this common ground with the men of Athens?

::EPICUREANS, STOICS, AND RUN-OF-THE-MILL IDOLATERS
When Paul addressed his audience in Athens, he had to relate the gospel to a very diverse group. The Epicureans believed that the world was formed and flourished by accidental material causes. The gods, if they existed at all, were thought to be, as Lucretius wrote, "far removed and withdrawn from our concerns . . . not wanting aught from us."[1]

The Stoics were pantheists who stressed the primacy of reason and civic duty. In the words of Marcus Aurelius, a man should take care "of this only all through life, that his thoughts turn not away from anything which belongs to an intelligent animal and a member of a civil community."[2]

In addition to these schools of thought, Athens was also filled with average citizens who worshiped a host of different deities.

2. Lest there be confusion, Paul wasn't encouraging polytheism in Athens. In what ways did he characterize the Unknown God, whom the Athenians worshiped in ignorance? (See Acts 17:22-34.)

3. According to Paul, the diversity and distribution of human society was not an accidental arrangement. How does he explain God's divine intention in ordering human societies just as they are?

::A GOOD JUDGMENT?

At the Tower of Babel, God miraculously diversified human language and dispersed humanity across the globe. The earth could not have sustained such a concentration of sinful men on "a plain in the land of Shinar" (Genesis 11:2), so God confused the common tongue and separated men into various people groups. Paul provides missionary insight into this judgment when he declares that God situated the people groups in their various homelands that they might seek Him.

4. What sort of response is warranted from those who have been introduced to the Unknown God?

5. Describe a time when you have found common ground with nonbelievers such that you were able to share the message of the gospel with them in terms they found accessible.

Ignoring the God who is known. If a person once admits he is a created being, not just a fortuitous combination of atoms, he must also face the question of how he should relate to his Creator. Until modern times, history has not held many philosophical atheists—those who deny the existence of God. However, Paul indicates in Romans 1:18-32 that there have always been many practical atheists—those who acknowledge God's existence yet ignore their responsibility to Him.

6. What does Paul say that all people can learn about God from observing the creation?

7. Imagine yourself as someone who has never read the Bible or heard about Jesus. What are some specific observations you could make about God from your experience of living in His world?

8. Consider Romans 1:21-23 and describe the route of regression people take from God when they ignore His attributes and suppress His truth.

::DENY THE ROOT, DESTROY THE FRUIT

The following is cited in Abraham Cohen's *Everyman's Talmud*: "On one occasion it is related, [Rabbi] Reuben stayed in Tiberias, and a philosopher asked him: 'Who is the most hateful person in the world?' 'The person who denies his Creator,' was the reply. 'How is that?' the philosopher asked; and the Rabbi answered: 'Honour thy father and thy mother; thou shalt not murder; thou shalt not commit adultery; thou shalt not steal; thou shalt not bear false witness against thy neighbor; thou shalt not covet — behold a person does not repudiate any of these laws until he repudiates the root of them (viz. God Who ordained them); and nobody proceeds to commit a transgression without first having denied Him Who prohibited it' (Tosifta Shebuoth III. 6)."[3]

9. Take note in the Romans 1 passage that God is still active in the lives of people who want nothing to do with Him. What kind of worship, beliefs, and behavior does God give them over to?

10. Paul begins this passage (1:18) by claiming that people suppress truths about God that they can readily learn from creation. He ends the chapter (1:32) by claiming that people may actually reach an extremity of corruption where they celebrate the very wickedness they know should be condemned. Take Paul's catalog of sins in 1:29-31 and give an example of how one of these sins, such as greed or strife, is celebrated in our culture today.

Trusting in the Lord who sustains. God did not merely wind up the universal clock millennia ago and step back to watch it wind down. The One who created the universe also "upholds all things by the word of His power" (Hebrews 1:3). In Colossians 1:15-20, Paul gave a window into the position that Jesus occupies and the power He exerts in the creative maintenance of the universe.

11. What do you think Paul signified in calling Jesus the "firstborn of all creation" (1:15)?

:: **WHEN YOUR WORLD GETS ROCKED**

Paul likely sent his letter to the Colossians in the early 60s AD, just a few years before a disastrous earthquake hit the area where Laodicea and Colossae stood. Several historians believe that Colossae was so devastated by this earthquake that no one ever undertook to rebuild it. In the face of such destruction and dislocation, it was vital for the Christians in that city to understand Paul's message that "everything, absolutely everything . . . . got started in [Jesus] and finds its purpose in him. He was there before any of it came into existence and holds it all together right up to this moment" (Colossians 1:16-17, MSG).

12. Describe the relationships Paul observed between

a. Jesus and the created order

b. Jesus and the Father

c. Jesus and the church (His new creation)

13. Much of our anxiety in life stems from the belief that things are happening around us that we cannot control or regulate to our benefit. If this is what we think, we are probably right, for we have very little direct control over life's circumstances.

Does this thought prompt greater anxiety in you? What kind of difference does it make that "all things hold together" in Jesus?

14. Describe one past experience that made you wonder, even briefly, if God was really holding all things together. Next, describe one past experience that confirmed for you that God is in control.

Worshiping the Lord who reigns. From the island of Patmos where the apostle John was exiled, he saw a vision of God reigning in heaven. The magnitude of the vision laid him on his face, but a resplendent Jesus lifted him up to receive a message for several churches in Asia Minor (modern-day Turkey). After this, we learn from Revelation 4:1-11 that John was actually called into the courts of heaven.

15. Describe the scene John saw in the courts of heaven. To what does he liken the appearance of God? How does he portray the physical environment around God's throne? What kind of company does God keep in heaven?

:: ON THE TESTIMONY OF THREE WITNESSES

We have reason to suspect that Paul saw a vision similar to the one John recorded in Revelation. Paul was "caught up to the third heaven . . . into Paradise and heard inexpressible words, which a man is not permitted to speak" (2 Corinthians 12:2-4). Centuries before, Isaiah had seen "the Lord sitting on a throne, lofty and exalted, with the train of His robe filling the temple" (Isaiah 6:1). On the testimony of these three witnesses, we may confidently expect to witness the angelic worship and hear the transcendent words of a heavenly court on the day that the Creator of this present world sets it aside to inaugurate a new age.

16. Though writing under divine inspiration, John must have found it quite an effort to describe what he saw in heaven. Identify three words or phrases from Revelation 4 that best capture the impression John's vision makes on you.

17. After setting the scene of the heavenly court, John described the kind of worship that is fitting in the presence of God. For which of God's *attributes* do the four creatures praise Him in Revelation 4:8? For which of His *acts* do the twenty-four elders praise Him in verse 11?

18. The book of Revelation makes it plain that the foundation of the world ages ago and the consummation of the ages in times to come fall under the jurisdiction of God. How does this understanding move you to worship or obey the God who holds creation in His hands?

AN OLD TESTAMENT EXCURSION

Humanity's place in the great void. Because scientists have crafted powerful telescopes in our modern era, we can look at distant galaxies in space and marvel at how relatively small the earth is. (How much smaller is a person, living on this insignificant rock orbiting a dying star!) Would it surprise you to learn that King David wrote Psalm 8 about this very experience more than 3,000 years ago?

1. Characterize the impression the heavens made on David as he gazed into the night sky.

2. What conclusion did David reach regarding man's place in God's creation? From where does he derive this conclusion?

3. How does worship envelop this meditation on the vastness of space and the glory of man?

::VOID OF UNDERSTANDING

Modern people are encouraged to feel insignificant against the backdrop of the limitless, empty expanse beyond earth's horizon. But since when did the mass or magnitude of a thing determine its worth? Is an elephant of greater value than a man because it is bigger and heavier? Or, as C. S. Lewis asked, "[Is a] taller man slightly more valuable than [a] shorter one?"[4] Then what cause do we have for looking at the vastness of the universe and concluding that man must be insignificant in the eyes of the Creator? Perhaps we should say, along with G. K. Chesterton, "I do not believe in dwelling upon the distances that are supposed to dwarf the world; I think there is even something a trifle vulgar about this idea of trying to rebuke spirit by size."[5]

4. Psalm 19 is a poetic reflection on the divine testimony written in the heavens and in the Word. Take note of how the psalmist characterized each witness and how we might benefit from their testimony. Be sure to note any contrasts you observe between the two witnesses.

THE WITNESS OF THE HEAVENS	THE WITNESS OF THE WORD

REFLECTIONS

Weeds, wind, and pigeons across the way. "Go to the ant, O sluggard" (Proverbs 6:6). That was Solomon's advice to his son who needed to learn diligence.

"Consider the lilies, how they grow," (Luke 12:27) Jesus told His anxious audience one day. Later He would instruct His disciples to "learn the parable of the fig tree" (Mark 13:28).

God may have a message for you from His creation. Are you listening? How could you do so more intently? Do you worry that such a thing might lead you to worship nature? You are probably in no great danger of this if you will also listen to the witness of the Spirit, the Scriptures, and the church. They are all pointing you toward the manifest grace of God in Jesus.

For most Christians, the danger lies not in paying too much

attention to nature but too little. A holy appreciation of God's world generates wonder and creativity in us, who are made in the Creator's image.

1. Take an object or process in the natural world around you and consider what you could learn from it. Feel free to correlate these observations to the teachings of Scripture. In the space below, write out the principle God wants you to learn from the weed growing in your garden, the wind stirring through your open window, or the bird perched on your neighbor's gutter. With whom could you share this parable in the coming week? (If there are children in your life, you might start with them!)

Is there room at the table? The Christian community today vigorously debates the age of the earth. Are the findings of most scientists, secular and religious, to be trusted? If so, we are living on a planet that is billions of years old, and we must concede that this figure fits uneasily into the framework of Genesis 1.

On the other hand, should we trust the scientists who propose a "young earth" model? Their cosmic chronology fits well with the Genesis record but uneasily into the geologic and chemical data as interpreted by the larger scientific community.

If you do not keep current on debates about the earth's age, consider that proponents of the contrasting models have very little respect for the viewpoints of those on the other side.

1. How vital is this debate to you? How vital is it to the Christian fellowship in which you participate? Are there dissenting views held within your church on the age of the earth?

2. If this topic were unimportant in the faith community, it probably would not be discussed at all. (Consider, by way of contrast, how many specifically Christian books have been written in the past decade to defend the particle theory of light.) What is at stake in the Christian community by deciding the question of the age of the earth one way or the other?

3. Do you believe there is or should be room for dissenting views about the earth's age among Bible teachers?

4. What steps could you take to better acquaint yourself with the viewpoints on both sides of this debate?

INTERSECTIONS

Let the Bible speak for itself. The Bible was not written to satisfy our curiosity; however, a person's curiosity might be just the thing that compels him or her to read the Bible. Many people in our culture know about the story of Adam and Eve and the apple, but very few have read it for themselves. (Of these, many would be surprised to find that Eve may have been tempted with an orange or a pear!)

Could it be that a friend or family member would be willing to read the first three chapters of Genesis with you if you asked? Here are six steps you could take to set up a profitable reading time together:

- Invite your friend or family member to read the first chapter of Genesis with you at a mutually agreeable time.
- Ahead of time read the chapter yourself, taking a lot of marginal notes as you go and turning them into several discussion-oriented questions.
- When you read the chapter with your friend, begin with three ground rules: (a) The text of Genesis will be the only source drawn from; (b) the goal will be to understand the meaning of the text, not to believe or disbelieve it; and (c) the answer "I don't know" will be preferred to a groundless guess.
- Read the chapter and let your questions (and the discussion) fly.
- Repeat with chapters 2 and 3.

The lessons of nature. The great mathematician and philosopher Blaise Pascal reveled in the grandeur of God's creation. He considered it a singular mark of the majesty of God. Yet he also observed the "astounding fact that no canonical writer has ever made use of nature to prove God."[6] The attempt to do so is fraught with problems.

1. What valid inferences do you think a nonbeliever could draw from observing nature?

2. What are some missteps a person might make in seeking to understand the nature of God through observations about the heavens, the earth, and the creatures on it?

The apostle Paul did not suggest in Romans 1 that a nonbeliever can read the book of nature on his own and understand all there is to know about God. Rather, he asserted "that which is known about God is evident within them; *for God made it evident to them*" (Romans 1:19, emphasis added). In other words, Paul insisted that God must give—and people must receive—the understanding needed to see God's eternal power and divine nature in the creation.

3. Describe some ways that a person could derive a system of false worship by mistaking "the voice of nature" for the voice of God in nature.

LAY IT TO YOUR HEART

Meditate on the following passages and commit them to memory:

- You established the earth, and it stands. They stand this day according to Your ordinances, for all things are Your servants. (Psalm 119:90-91)
- For us there is but one God, the Father, from whom are all things and we exist for Him; and one Lord, Jesus Christ, by whom are all things, and we exist through Him. (1 Corinthians 8:6)
- Worthy are You, our Lord and our God, to receive glory and honor and power; for You created all things, and because of Your will they existed, and were created. (Revelation 4:11)

A POLLUTED SOURCE

SIN FLOWS FROM WITHIN ::

" I 've got good news, and I've got bad news. Which do you want first?"

How many conversations have begun with those words? If you're like me, you'd rather have no bad news at all. But if that's not an option, better to get the bad news out of the way first and save the good news for last.

You might say the Bible respects this human preference. Or perhaps God Himself endowed us with this preference to make us ready for the gospel. We live with a heaviness about the sin within and hope for some solution from above. This is the inescapable bad news we hear first from our conscience.

"It is a thing rooted in the origins," said G. K. Chesterton. "Whatever else men have believed, they have all believed there is something the matter with mankind."[1]

When we open the Bible where it actually begins, in the book of Genesis, we learn that God created man in His image in a verdant garden of divine harmony. Nevertheless, man exercised the power of free will, implicit in the divine image, to rebel against his Creator. Thus, God sent humans into physical and spiritual exile. Adam and Eve were banished from the Garden of Eden and became subject to evil inclinations they were powerless to resist.

That was the bad news. But the good news came hard on its heels.

God showered Adam and Eve with immediate and ongoing mercy from the time He evicted them from Eden. What is more, He instructed their offspring in His rules for right conduct and promised them a Redeemer who would be born among them to destroy the Evil One.

This was, indeed, good news. But the ugly truth remained. Something had altered within humanity at the Fall, and sublime laws—even divine laws—could not effect a change of heart and give man the power consistently to choose righteousness even when he knew it to be right.

It would be hard to overstate the continuity between this picture of sin drawn up in the Old Testament and the teachings that develop it in the New Testament. It would be impossible to overstate the importance of both of these in preparing man to receive the good news.

The message that "all have sinned and fall short of the glory of God" (Romans 3:23) is not a pleasant one to hear or to preach. No one likes to contemplate this bad news, and fewer like to proclaim it. But if the bad news can't be avoided, better to have out with it straightaway and follow it up with the good news. Better to receive the diagnosis, be it ever so hard to hear, so that we can seek an adequate cure as quickly as possible.

The "good news"—that is a literal translation of the Greek term we typically render "gospel"—will never be received as truly good until we understand the gravity of the news that is really bad. That is the message about the sin condition of man, to which we turn in this study.

A GUIDED EXPEDITION

The spring of sin. In Jesus' day, devout Jews were extremely scrupulous about eating only foods that were ritually clean. They would avoid certain foods altogether and carefully ensure all others were prepared in appropriate vessels with clean utensils. As we see in Mark 7:14-23, Jesus drew upon this religious tradition to challenge the people in His day to think deeply about the nature of uncleanness.

1. To whom did Jesus address His words in this passage?

2. Why do you suppose Jesus' disciples were confused by His teaching?

::THE TRADITIONS OF THE ELDERS

Mark records that "the Pharisees and all the Jews do not eat unless they carefully wash their hands, thus observing *the traditions of the elders*" (Mark 7:3, emphasis added). The Pharisees asked why Jesus' disciples did not "walk according to the tradition of the elders" (7:5). Jesus rebuked the Pharisees for "setting aside the commandment of God in order to keep your tradition" (7:9). These traditions were not a fuzzy set of teachings but a well-developed body of biblical interpretation and application known as the oral law. It was held to be as authoritative as the written Old Testament. The traditions of the elders, the oral law, were eventually recorded in the compilation known as the Mishnah. It was over this oral tradition that Jesus ran afoul of the Pharisees most often in His public ministry.

3. Describe the tone of Jesus' response to the disciples when they asked Him to explain His meaning. Why did He respond in this way?

4. According to Jesus, where do evil behaviors like sexual immorality, envy, and pride originate?

5. It has been said that the line between childhood and adulthood lies somewhere between "The plate broke" and "I broke the plate." If only things were so simple. A cursory examination of our own lives reveals that we still try to shift the blame for our faults onto circumstances or other people. How have you struggled with the inclination to shift blame for sins (like dishonesty or envy) onto something or someone else?

The struggle within. Have you ever experienced the inward tug-of-war between a desire to do what you know is right on one hand and the desire to do something clearly wrong on the other? If so, then Romans 7:18–8:4 will seem more like autobiography than theology to you. In it, Paul describes the spiritual condition of a person who lives with an awareness of the righteous standard of God but without the consistent willpower to carry it out.

6. According to Paul, what resources does the flesh offer a person who wants to live according to God's righteous standards? Describe a real circumstance in which you have sincerely tried to carry out God's command in your own strength.

7. What law (or principle) is at work in the heart of a person who is struggling to choose right and refuse wrong? From where does this law derive its authority? Does it operate chiefly on the mind, the desires, or the will?

:: A HIGHER POWER

In Romans 7, Paul describes the plight of a Christian who finds himself incompetent to obey the divine Law, even though he believes it to be good and godly to do so. He simply doesn't have the power in himself to overcome the sin rooted in his flesh. That is why Romans 8 develops like the dawn of a new world, where man actually finds access to the kind of strength he needs to live a holy life. Where does this strength come from? As Bible teacher John MacArthur says, "The Spirit, who was mentioned only once in chapters 1–7 (cf.1:4), is referred to nearly 20 times in chapter 8."[2] The indwelling presence of the Holy Spirit gives a Christian the spiritual power to abide by "the righteous requirement of the law" (Romans 8:4, ESV).

8. What assurance does Romans 8:1 offer a person whose decisions and life choices have been adversely affected by the law of sin within? In what ways has God intervened to set us free from the law of sin at work within us?

9. Most Christians who have sincerely endeavored to live a godly life have encountered some sinful habit of thought or life that simply will not submit to the rule of righteousness. Describe the struggle you have had with such an entrenched sin. Did your resolution to be holy suffer any setbacks as you saw how difficult it would be to live free of this sin? Were you ever tempted to call an uneasy truce with the habit and let it command some small corner of your life? From this passage in Romans, what hope is offered to those of us who wonder whether sinful habits must inevitably drag us down?

The living dead. In Ephesians 2:1-7, Paul piles one assertion on top of another to describe our spiritual condition apart from Christ. He begins with the pointed claim, "You were dead in the trespasses and sins in which you once walked" (2:1-2, ESV).

10. In what sense can Paul say that a person living in sin is actually *dead*?

11. Describe what kind of influence each of the following exerts on the life of a person living in transgressions and sins:

The course of this world

The prince of the power of the air

The desires of our flesh

The desires of our mind

12. Characterize the way God relates to people who are dead in transgressions and sins.

::THE TWO-WORD SYNOPSIS

While many people consider Romans the fullest development of Paul's theology and Ephesians the capstone of his catholic letters, the heart of Paul's teaching can be summed up in two words: "in Christ." Paul uses this expression (or an equivalent such as "in Him") more than fifteen times in the first two chapters of Ephesians to signify that God reckons us so united with Christ that His righteous life, atoning death, and triumphant resurrection are our own. In light of this unfathomable gain, Paul claims that his sole aim is to "gain Christ, and may be found in Him, not having a righteousness of my own derived from the Law, but that which is through faith in Christ" (Philippians 3:8-9).

Trials and temptations. Suppose you take your car in for routine maintenance and find it requires a major repair. It's the end of the month and your checking account long ago surrendered ground to your credit card. You discover that a coworker, slightly better-looking and totally underqualified, received a promotion you were eligible for. On top of all this, you feel a cold coming on. How do you inwardly respond to difficulties like this? And where do these inward responses originate? That is the subject of James' reflection in his letter (see James 1:12-17).

13. According to James, what role does God play in tempting you during the trials of life?

14. What distinction can be drawn legitimately between a trial and a temptation?

15. Where do temptations originate, and where are they headed?

16. Bearing in mind the principle of James 1:17, what deception do you think James is warning us to avoid in verse 16?

:: THE FATE OF JAMES

"Blessed is a man who perseveres under trial," James wrote (1:12). These words could ring hollow — like a shallow pep talk — if they came from the lips of a man enjoying comfortable circumstances. James, however, lived a life that lent credibility to his teaching. According to the ancient writers Clement, Josephus, and Hegesippus, James was held in highest regard among the Jews in Jerusalem. Hegesippus relates that James "was in the habit of entering the temple alone and was often found upon his bended knees, and interceding for the forgiveness of the people [i.e. the Jewish people]; so that his knees became as hard as a camel's, in consequence of his habitual supplication and kneeling before God."[3] James met his end in martyrdom, when he was thrown down the temple steps, stoned, and bludgeoned to death with a fuller's club.

17. Describe one particular time when a sinful inclination took hold in your heart as a trial evolved (or erupted) in your world? How did you justify your sinful reaction initially? When did you begin to face up to the wrongness of your inward response? What lessons have you carried away from the experience?

AN OLD TESTAMENT EXCURSION

As we have seen, the New Testament writers stressed the presence and influence of sin on the inside of man, not simply in the world around us. This doctrine didn't originate in the New Testament, though. It was there all along—throughout the Old Testament—as a consistent reminder that man must not search for salvation within himself but in relationship with God.

1. Choose three of the following Old Testament passages and comment on what you learn from these about the origin, scope, and/or influence of sin.

   ▪ Then the LORD saw that the wickedness of man was great on the earth, and that every intent of the thoughts of his heart was only evil continually. (Genesis 6:5)

   ▪ What is man, that he should be pure, or he who is born of a woman, that he should be righteous? Behold, [God] puts no trust in His holy ones, and the heavens are not pure in His sight; how much less one who is detestable and corrupt, Man, who drinks iniquity like water! (Job 15:14-16)

■ The LORD has looked down from heaven upon the sons of men to see if there are any who understand, who seek after God. They have all turned aside, together they have become corrupt; there is no one who does good, not even one. (Psalm 14:2-3)

■ Behold, I was brought forth in iniquity, and in sin my mother conceived me. (Psalm 51:5)

■ Watch over your heart with all diligence, for from it flow the springs of life. (Proverbs 4:23)

■ Who can say, "I have cleansed my heart, I am pure from my sin"? (Proverbs 20:9)

■ He who trusts in his own heart is a fool, but he who walks wisely will be delivered. (Proverbs 28:26)

- Indeed, there is not a righteous man on earth who continually does good and who never sins. (Ecclesiastes 7:20)

- This is an evil in all that is done under the sun, that there is one fate for all men. Furthermore, the hearts of the sons of men are full of evil and insanity is in their hearts throughout their lives. Afterwards they go to the dead. (Ecclesiastes 9:3)

- All of us like sheep have gone astray, each of us has turned to his own way; but the LORD has caused the iniquity of us all to fall on Him. (Isaiah 53:6)

- The heart is more deceitful than all else and is desperately sick; who can understand it? (Jeremiah 17:9)

REFLECTIONS

Firsthand observations from the frontlines. Not all temptations wield the same influence equally on all people. In *Surprised by Joy*, C. S. Lewis describes quite vividly the homosexual practices in his boarding school and imagines some of his readers objecting that he doesn't condemn "the heinousness of the sin." Lewis responds by declaring that homosexuality and gambling were the only two sins he never felt tempted to commit. They were "enemies [he] had never met in battle,"[4] so he declined to say much about them.

Like Lewis, we are not equally tempted to commit every sin, and we should be wary of condemning the sins of others when we have not walked a mile in their shoes. Even so, all of us do have our own battles to wage. About the frontlines we fight on, we can speak quite personally and knowledgeably.

1. What sinful inclinations have exerted themselves most strenuously within you?

2. How is your battle within affected (for good or ill) by the circumstances around you?

3. In what ways does your own mental and physical well-being play into your struggle against sin?

4. Have you witnessed the declining power of certain temptations in the course of your life? What accounts for the change?

The decisive victory and the daily skirmishes. The advent of Christ spelled the downfall of sin. In a certain respect, it is just that simple. As John wrote, "The Son of God appeared for this purpose, to destroy the works of the devil" (1 John 3:8). But "the works of the devil" have not been finally driven from our hearts.

Our own experience—and the experience of even the most revered Christians—assures us that Christ's decisive victory over Satan must somehow be applied to our daily skirmishes with sin.

5. What power does sin now exert over the life of a Christian? In what respect can we claim to be "dead to sin"? How can a person slough off sinful habits? Choose whichever of these questions interests you most and compose a provisional answer to it after reflecting on the relevant Scripture(s):

   ■ In what respect is a Christian dead to sin? (Romans 6:4-14)

   ■ Shouldn't a Christian live a sinless life? (1 John 1:5–2:2)

   ■ How does a Christian put off the old self? (Ephesians 4:20-24; Colossians 3:1-9)

INTERSECTIONS

Another point of view. Interview a good friend who is not a Christian and ask that person to talk you through his or her beliefs about the origin of evil. You might introduce the topic by telling him that you've been studying what the Bible has to say. Be prepared to open and carry along the informal interview with questions like, "How would you define evil? Where do you think evil originated? What are some of the best responses we can make to the problem of evil?" You might also be prepared to give a synopsis of what you've learned in your study, in case you're asked.

The role of hypocrisy. Sometimes, we lack a certain proportion in addressing the bad news about sin in ourselves and in our society. That is, we tend to focus our attention on the desperate evil of certain sins in others, while excusing an unholy host of "smaller" ones that we may cherish. (For example, we justly feel that child abuse is horrible, even criminal, but we manage to justify our own harsh words to our children.)

In short, we are hypocrites. We condemn sins beyond a certain threshold or in certain people, yet condone them on another level in ourselves. We are all laid open to Paul's charge, "You . . . who teach another, do you not teach yourself?" (Romans 2:21).

1. Often we see this kind of hypocrisy plague the church. But what about yourself? What kind of response does your hypocrisy as a Christian elicit from nonbelievers?

2. What steps could you and your Christian fellowship take to turn your specific hypocrisy on its head?

LAY IT TO YOUR HEART

Meditate on the following passages and commit them to memory:
- There is no one who does good, not even one. (Psalm 14:3)
- Indeed, there is not a righteous man on earth who continually does good and who never sins. (Ecclesiastes 7:20)
- There is no distinction; for all have sinned and fall short of the glory of God, being justified as a gift by His grace through the redemption which is in Christ Jesus. (Romans 3:22-24)

AN OPEN INVITATION

GOD WELCOMES ALL NATIONS TO BECOME HIS PEOPLE ::

When you distill the Bible down to its essence, it is a book about relationships. Many people who set out to read it from cover to cover get lost in Leviticus and conclude it's a book about laws. Others stall out in Chronicles and think of it as a book about ancient history. Almost everyone makes forays into the Psalms and Proverbs, and they leave thinking the Old Testament is a book about lofty ideals and practical wisdom.

Undoubtedly, all these impressions are true. The Bible is a compilation of laws and lofty ideals, of history and wisdom. However, the Bible is not merely that. It is the story of God's love for His creation — and particularly for those creatures called humans. You can test this theory by opening up to the first pages of Genesis and the last pages of Revelation.

In the beginning, you find God creating a world by His might and for His pleasure. In this new world, He placed Adam and Eve, people who were made in His image, who walked together with Him in the cool of the day.

The last pages of Revelation do not end with the apocalyptic visions of our modern media. Instead, the story ends with a new civilization, a new city that God has prepared and over which He pronounces: "Behold, the tabernacle of God is among men, and He will dwell among them, and they shall be His people, and God Himself will be among them, and He will wipe away every tear from their eyes; and there will no longer be any death; there will no longer be any mourning, or crying, or pain; the first things have passed away. . . . Behold, I am making all things new" (Revelation 21:3-5).

If a person loses sight of this larger picture, the Bible can become a labyrinth of laws and literature. We must keep the whole picture in view: The Bible is a story about relationship!

From the second chapter of Genesis to the second-to-last chapter of Revelation, however, the story has to do with a strained relationship. Man rejected the love of God and chose to walk out of Eden into sin. The whole of the Bible is a detailed account of God's relentless efforts to restore man to the divine relationship for which he was created.

But how would God do this work of restoration? A seer might have anticipated the answer, but most of us could never have guessed it. To save the entire world, God chose one man.

Abraham was not endowed with great potential for this task. At that time, he had no children, nor even a home of his own. He was wealthy enough, but his riches seemed irrelevant to his destiny. What mattered was that Abraham had faith in God. This was the asset God had given him and which He intended to multiply until the riches of grace spilled over onto "all the families of the earth" (Genesis 12:3).

With marvelous irony, God determined to save the entire world by choosing one man and through His descendants, one Messiah. At the arrival of Jesus, the door of salvation swung wide to the world. But make no mistake, God still chooses His people one at a time.

A GUIDED EXPEDITION

Many from the east and the west. Jesus did not travel much beyond the borders of Israel during His time on earth, nor did He have fellowship with Gentiles as He did with other Jews. However, the gospel writers made a point to highlight several of Jesus' interactions with Gentiles living within or adjacent to the land of Israel. Matthew 8:5-13 records just such an encounter.

1. According to this text, why did the Roman centurion (a Gentile) seek out Jesus? How would you describe the centurion's character?

2. Characterize the impression this centurion made on Jesus. (It is the same impression His own townspeople made on Him in Mark 6:1-6, but to a much different effect.) For what reason did Jesus commend the centurion?

:: THE GOOD "BAD GUYS"

In the first century, each centurion commanded one hundered or so soldiers throughout Israel and other Roman territories. Although not all centurions were of Roman extraction, they were all Gentiles and comprised an unwelcomed occupying force in Israel. Nevertheless, the centurions we encounter in the New Testament are all presented in a favorable light. A centurion at the cross confesses that Jesus is the Son of God (see Matthew 27:54). Cornelius, a centurion in Caesarea, is one of the first Gentiles to receive the gospel (see Acts 10). And Paul's life is spared en route to Rome when a centurion prevents his soldiers from executing all the prisoners on board his sinking ship (see Acts 27).

3. Jesus capitalized on the centurion's response, recorded in Matthew 8:9, to teach an emphatic lesson about who will enjoy fellowship with the Jewish patriarchs — Abraham, Isaac, and Jacob — in the kingdom of heaven. Do you suppose the centurion himself would be included? How do you think Jesus would have responded if someone in the crowd had protested, "But these people You are speaking about are not even Jews"?

4. Toward which people might Jesus be directing your attention with the words, "Many will come from east and west" (Matthew 8:11)? Do some of these people who seem so far away from the gospel live within your community? If so, how could you reach out to them? If not, how might you demonstrate the kind of concern for them that Jesus has?

The Jews, the Gentiles, and Jesus. In the Old Testament God chose the nation of Israel to be "a people for His own possession out of all the peoples who are on the face of the earth" (Deuteronomy 7:6). Yet the door of salvation swung open to the whole world—Gentiles and Jews—in the New Testament. Does that mean the Jews no longer stand in unique relation to God? Or does it mean that Gentiles are second-class citizens of God's kingdom, reserved principally for Jews? The church wrestled with both options during its formative years, and Paul tackles the topic head-on in Romans 11.

5. According to the first verses of Romans 11, describe the relationship God maintains with the Jewish people?

6. What lesson for the present time did Paul observe in the story of Elijah, who once believed himself the only Jew on earth who still worshiped the Lord (see 1 Kings 18–19)?

7. Why did the Jewish people in New Testament times fail to obtain the salvation they were seeking?

8. What lesson did Paul intend his Gentile audience to understand from the analogies about the dough and the root in Romans 11:16-24?

9. When Paul called the relation between the Jews, the Gentiles, and Jesus a "mystery" in Romans 11:25, he did not mean it is an incomprehensible enigma. Rather, he meant that we could never have anticipated or invented this truth apart from the divine revelation of Scriptures and the divine incarnation of Christ. Now, however, this mystery has been made plain. How would you describe it in your own words?

:: PAUL'S USE OF THE TERM MYSTERY

Paul used the word mystery twenty times in his letters, often to denote "some sacred thing hidden or secret which is naturally unknown to human reason and is only known by the revelation of God."[1] While a sane Christian should never claim to know all the mysteries of God, neither should that person surrender the claim that God has revealed a part of His mysterious will in His written Word. We come to understand the message of salvation by grace through faith in Christ alone not by philosophical inquiry, personal introspection, or natural observation but by receiving the Word which God has revealed. God's will "is not in heaven, that you should say, 'Who will go up to heaven for us to get it for us and make us hear it, that we may observe it?' Nor is it beyond the sea that you should say, 'Who will cross the sea for us to get it for us and make us hear it, that we may observe it?' But the word is very near you" (Deuteronomy 30:12-14).

10. Consider the transition from theological reflection to spontaneous worship that takes place in Romans 11:32-33. Now that you have considered the same truths that tuned Paul's heart to praise, turn your own pen toward prayer. What would you like to say to God about His wisdom in making a way for Gentiles to be saved without alienating the Jews? What about His mercy in choosing you? Write out your own prayer of gratitude to God.

Strangers at home. By the middle of the first century, the gospel had moved forward into many communities of the Mediterranean world. No longer just a Jewish sect, Christianity had become an international religion. In Peter's letter to the Christians in Asia Minor, he connected the Gentile experience of forsaking pagan traditions with the Jewish experience of exile and refers to the whole congregation as "aliens" and "strangers" in the places they called home (see 1 Peter 1:1; 2:11).

11. What observations do you make about each of the following from 1 Peter 2:4-12?

   ■ "A living stone . . . a precious corner stone" (see also Psalm 118:22; Isaiah 8:14-15; 28:16).

   ■ "Living stones."

   ■ The purpose of the "spiritual house."

12. List the four ways Peter identified the church in verse 9, and comment on the significance of each description.

::**KEEPING THE END IN VIEW**

When God selected Abraham and his descendants to be His special possession, He was not playing favorites among the people of the earth. Rather, He was choosing the best means for saving them. Out of His goodness, God desired Adam's whole family to be redeemed, and out of His wisdom, He chose Abraham's family to do it. It is only when we mistake God's means for His ends that the notion of being chosen by God begins to sound elitist. God chose you because He loves you and wants to save you, to be sure. But He didn't choose you in order to shun other people; instead, He chose you to "proclaim the excellencies of Him who has called you out of darkness into His marvelous light" (1 Peter 2:9).

13. According to 1 Peter 2:9-12, what kind of ministry and integrity should characterize God's chosen people?

14. Describe some dangers that develop when a Christian begins to feel at home in a culture where he is really a stranger.

AN OLD TESTAMENT EXCURSION

The Messiah's ministry to all nations. Although the Scriptures declare that Israel was God's "treasured possession among all peoples . . . a kingdom of priests and a holy nation" (Exodus 19:5-6, ESV), the Old Testament also forecasts a time when all the nations would enter into a similar relationship with God because of the ministry of the Messiah. Psalm 22 is a messianic prophecy about the sufferings and glory of Jesus.

1. Describe the comparisons you observe between the descriptions from Psalm 22:1-18 and the story of Jesus' crucifixion.

2. According to verses 19-26, what would be the repercussion of Jesus' suffering and restoration among His "brethren" (Israel)?

3. How will the "ends of the earth" (verses 27-31) be impacted by the ministry of the Messiah?

Blessed to be a blessing. Perhaps you attend a church where your pastor ends the service by pronouncing this blessing over the congregation: "The LORD bless you, and keep you; the LORD make His face shine on you, and be gracious to you; the LORD lift up His countenance on you, and give you peace" (Numbers 6:24-26).

Certainly, the people of Israel were familiar with this refrain, for by it, the priests would invoke God's blessing over His people. Yet why should God choose to bless Israel? Everyone knew that it was for their good and because of His love, but did His care for one nation have implications for all nations?

4. What insight does Psalm 67 offer to this question?

5. What are the implications for your life, as well?

::GOOD NEWS FOR THE OVERLOOKED

If you've ever had the humiliating experience of being chosen last for a game of kickball on a school playground, the gospel should resound in your ears as truly good news. "God has chosen the foolish things of the world . . . the weak things of the world . . . and the base things of the world and the despised God has chosen, the things that are not" (1 Corinthians 1:27-28). It may be humbling to think that God directs His saving mercy to the weak and foolish, but such a thought rings true with the Scriptures. For "all flesh is grass, and all its loveliness is like the flower of the field. The grass withers, the flower fades, when the breath of the LORD blows upon it; surely the people are grass. The grass withers, the flower fades, but the word of our God stands forever" (Isaiah 40:6-8). Thus, the Victorian poet Francis Thompson could write, "I am as God; alas, / And such a god of grass! / A little root clay-caught, / A wind, a flame, a thought, / Inestimably naught!"[2]

REFLECTIONS

Chosen to be comfortable? It is easy to make the mental mistake of thinking that being chosen by God means being pampered by Him in this life. Real life usually scuttles this mistaken belief quickly. Real life cannot, however, supplant the mistaken belief with a true one. Only Scripture can do that.

1. What do you know about the hardships undergone by the following people? Choose two of them and answer the questions in each column.

GOD'S CHOSEN ONES	WHAT HARD-SHIPS DID THEY EXPERIENCE?	HOW WOULD YOU PROTEST TO GOD IF YOU WERE IN THEIR SHOES?	HOW DID GOD BRING GOOD OUT OF THEIR HARDSHIPS?
Joseph (Genesis 37; 39 — 45)			
Esther (Esther 2 — 8)			
Daniel (Daniel 1 — 2)			
Paul (1 Corinthians 11:23-33)			

Elected, predestined, or foreknown? When we tackle the topic of the "chosen people," we enter into an area occupied by two camps of theologians with different views about how God's sovereignty in saving people interacts with their responsibility to follow Him.

2. To get a handle on the broad outline of the debate, consider the chart below and write down your own questions or objections to both positions.

	CALVINISTS (OR REFORMED)	ARMINIANS
Summary of General Beliefs	Before the foundation of the world, God decreed: • that some people would be saved and that these would definitely respond to His offer of salvation. • that some would not be saved and would be punished for their rejection of Jesus.	Before the foundation of the world, God looked ahead into human history and saw who would believe in Jesus and who would reject Him. The former, God elected to be saved, while the latter, He elected to be damned, according to the way He knew they would respond to Jesus.
Key Term	Predestination (or Election)	Foreknowledge
Key Scriptures	Romans 9:10-21; Ephesians 1:3-6	1 Timothy 2:5-6; 2 Peter 3:8-9; Revelation 22:17
What questions or objections do you raise against these beliefs?		

INTERSECTIONS

By word and deed. As God's children, we are called to declare His glories and demonstrate what life in His kingdom looks like. Yet we are often prone to withhold either our life's example or the message of God's excellencies from people around us who don't know God.

1. How have you kept this double-sided ministry of proclamation and presence in balance?

2. Where have you struggled most to maintain a balanced and persuasive witness?

3. What do you consider to be the perils of only talking to lost people about the gospel without sharing life together with them? What are the perils of only setting a good example but never opening your mouth?

A global community. Though the Christian church has been prominent in Western cultures since the Middle Ages, it is a mistake to regard it as a "Western" phenomenon. How do the following considerations influence your appreciation of the global nature of Christianity and the expansive love of Jesus?

1. The Jewish origins of Christianity.

2. The historic progression of Christianity from Jerusalem.

3. The current status of the church outside of Western countries.

4. The promise of Jesus in Matthew 8:5-13 and His command in 28:19-20.

LAY IT TO YOUR HEART

Meditate on the following passages and commit them to memory:

- I have other sheep, which are not of this fold; I must bring them also, and they will hear My voice; and they will become one flock with one shepherd. (John 10:16)
- For there is no distinction between Jew and Greek; for the same Lord is Lord of all, abounding in riches for all who call on Him. (Romans 10:12)
- But you are a chosen race, a royal priesthood, a holy nation, a people for God's own possession, so that you may proclaim the excellencies of Him who has called you out of darkness into His marvelous light. (1 Peter 2:9)

FREE AT LAST

WE ARE DELIVERED TO FULFILL OUR DESTINY ::

G od's signal act of deliverance in the Old Testament was the Exodus of Israel from Egypt. God took an oppressed nation of slaves, whom He had chosen for His children, and escorted them straight across the border of the mightiest empire in the world.

Ever after, the Exodus lived in the imaginations and sacred writings of the Jewish people as a hallmark of God's compassionate power: compassion for His suffering people who were too weak to deliver themselves, and power to accomplish His purposes in spite of the might and misdirection of men.

Even so, the Old Testament tips us off to a subtle and serious problem that plagued Israel five paces across the Red Sea on their way to the Promised Land. The people who had been freed from captivity in Egypt were still in bondage to sin.

Though they were walking away from a pagan nation, they were bringing along pagan gods to worship. And though they no longer heard the angry shouts of their Egyptian taskmasters, they had internalized the grumbling and complaining, so they constantly directed their bitterness against Moses and Aaron. In Egypt, the people genuinely believed God had forsaken them. En route to the Promised Land, their belief remained unshaken. In short, the yoke of external oppression had been broken, but the yoke of internal slavery remained. Israel's freedom from Egypt only served to reveal how deeply enslaved they were to sin.

If this were true of the children of God, how much more so of the nations who did not know or serve Him? How would God deal with this new, or newly revealed, slavery? How would He set His people free from their bondage within?

God began the task by giving Israel His Law (more on that in the next chapter) and assuring them that abiding by it would be their righteousness. Yet the Law, righteous as it was, stood outside the man, beckoning him to become someone he was not. It could instruct, correct, and condemn him for his behavior and beliefs. It could even provide instruction about how a condemned man might find atonement for his sins. But it could not break through the stronghold of sin that was fortified within his own heart. No instrument outside of man, be it ever so mighty, could break an internal bondage.

The Law being given, the question still remained: How could a man be set free from his internal bondage to sin to obey the Law? The only hint we have in the Old Testament is that God would someday do a work through the Messiah whereby He would change not only the terms of His covenant with Israel but Israel itself. And not only Israel. God actually promised He would change the world by changing the men who inhabited it.

This is the very heartbeat of the gospel. This is the New Testament teaching about deliverance. Man can find deliverance from his bondage to sin. In Christ, sin's power is broken within us and its penalty canceled in the heavenly court.

A GUIDED EXPEDITION

You must be born again. As all the gospel writers observe, Jesus initially enjoyed a time of great popularity among the Jewish people of His day—a popularity that waned but never evaporated completely. After all, a large crowd hailed Him as the Son of David when He entered Jerusalem for the last time, and the Pharisees had to arrest Him at night for fear of a popular backlash.

But Jesus never enjoyed much popularity among the religious leadership. The gospels record only a few constructive encounters with such leaders, and one of them is given in John 3:1-18.

1. Why do you suppose the Pharisee, Nicodemus, came to Jesus by night?

2. Weigh the statement that Nicodemus made to Jesus in verse 2 against the response he receives from Jesus in verse 3. What was Nicodemus saying in the first place? Was Jesus' response relevant?

3. When Nicodemus expresses his consternation with the words "unless one is born again he cannot see the kingdom of God," Jesus clarifies what this rebirth means by referencing Ezekiel 36:25-27. How do Ezekiel's words about "water" and "a new spirit" help you make sense of Jesus' teaching to Nicodemus?

:: THE EVOLUTION OF CHRISTIAN COURAGE

Nicodemus appears three times in the gospel of John. The first time, he approached Jesus by night to speak with Him privately about spiritual things. Next, we find Nicodemus voicing his opposition to the other Pharisees' hasty judgments against Jesus (see John 7:50-52). When we meet him for the final time (19:38-40), Nicodemus is working alongside Joseph of Arimathea, who was "a disciple of Jesus, but a secret one for fear of the Jews" (19:38), to anoint Jesus' body and place it in a tomb.

Though confused, Nicodemus wanted to know more about how this new birth would take place. Jesus declines the invitation to talk about "heavenly things," since Nicodemus is struggling to grasp the meaning of already revealed prophecy. However, Jesus informs him that eternal salvation will come like earthly salvation did in Moses' day.

4. How would you explain Jesus' teaching to a person who is unfamiliar with the reference to the serpents in Numbers 21:4-9?

5. Though Jesus refrained from talking with Nicodemus about "heavenly things," He still boiled down the gospel to a pure and memorable essence in John 3:16-18. From this passage, write out three things that are true about *God*, three that are true about the *world*, and three that are true about *you*.

Freedom beyond forgiveness. If God provides abundant grace where sin abounds, perhaps Christians should sin as much as possible to receive more grace from God. That logic probably bothers you, even if you've toyed with it in your worst moments. The thought of Christians sinning to give God more opportunities to forgive them seems, well, unchristian. Paul argues the very same thing in Romans 6:1-14.

6. Before you read Paul's arguments, offer one or two suggestions about how you would attempt to argue a friend out of a decision to plunge headlong into sin on the supposition that God will forgive him for it later?

7. Paul answers the hypothetical question, "Are we to continue in sin so that grace may increase?" with two rhetorical questions (verses 1-3). Turn these two questions into straightforward statements, and write them below.

:: BOTH SIDES OF DELIVERANCE

The coin of Christian deliverance has two sides: We are liberated from the dominion of sin and liberated to the power of righteousness. We are, in Paul's words, "rescued . . . from the domain of darkness, and transferred . . . to the kingdom of His beloved Son" (Colossians 1:13). We are not, as it were, set free from a prison of perpetual transgression and guilt, then left to wander about aimlessly trying to live the holy life that formerly eluded us. Rather, by God's grace through the indwelling Spirit, we can live the righteous life God requires. As author Jerry Bridges has said, "We have been given all we need to bring the imperative — 'do not let sin reign in your mortal body' — into line with the indicative — 'we died to sin.'"[1]

The New Testament teaches a radical union between Christ and a Christian. If you have trusted in Christ, God sees and receives you in Him. You could say that God so orders His will that Jesus actually stands in your place, receiving the punishment you should have received and living the life you could not have lived. It was so before you were a Christian, and it is so now. Paul goes so far as to claim that we are dead to sin because Christ died.

8. How would you define what it means to be dead to sin? In what ways have you experienced this death to sin?

::THIS GOOD NEWS REALLY IS NEW

In the realm of world religions, only Christianity offers a substantially different answer to the problem of sin. Most religions offer instruction about how we may overcome our sinful behavior to align ourselves with good or right or the will of God. Only in the gospel do we discover that God Himself came to earth to destroy the power of sin. He does not simply give us more and better information about deliverance, He incarnates Himself as the Savior and Deliverer.

9. Paul prioritizes our identity in Christ (Romans 6:1-11) ahead of our behavior as Christians (verses 12-14), as if *who we are* takes precedence over *what we ought to do*. It seems that believing what is true about ourselves makes it possible for us to behave in ways that are consistent with our identity. What are the implications of reversing Paul's teaching and dwelling first and foremost on what we ought to do for God rather than who we are in Christ?

Restoration to our destiny. If you look back to Eden, you find that humanity's original charter was to "be fruitful and multiply, and fill the earth, and subdue it; and rule over the fish of the sea and over the birds of the sky and over every living thing that moves on the earth" (Genesis

1:28). But how was man to rule over the whole creation after the Fall when he could not master his own evil inclinations? This very dilemma is tackled in Hebrews 2:5-18.

10. According to Hebrews 2:8, what disparity may we observe between God's original plan for man—his job description quoted from Psalm 8—and man's current condition?

11. The Father sent the Son that man might be redeemed from death to his original destiny. What reasons does the writer of Hebrews give for why Jesus suffered as a man? What effect did Jesus' sacrifice have on the Devil?

:: LAY DOWN THE BURDEN

In describing our deliverance from an internal bondage to sin, the writer of Hebrews declares that Christ's blood will "cleanse your conscience" (9:14; see also 10:22). Christ shed His blood on the cross "to put away sin by the sacrifice of Himself" (9:26). What Christ has put away, you have no right or reason to take up again. Lay your guilt aside, no matter how grave your past offenses, for Christ has been "offered once to bear the sins of many" (9:28).

12. Each verse in Hebrews 2:15-18 speaks of some benefit that comes to us as a result of Jesus' sufferings. List each one below, and comment on how God meets our needs through His Son—needs we cannot meet ourselves.

13. Our inward slavery to sin renders us impotent to carry out the plans God has for us. The work of ruling over creation is simply too heavy for a man weakened by sin. How have the sins of sexual lust, greed, bitterness, or the like weakened you for the work that God has entrusted to you? What promise does Hebrews 2:15-18 offer to those of us who have faltered or failed in ruling over our own sinful inclinations?

AN OLD TESTAMENT EXCURSION

Overmastered. Genesis 3 gives an account of Adam and Eve's first sin. Immediately after eating the forbidden fruit, they felt shame over their nakedness, hid from God's presence, and tried to shift the blame onto someone else. They were dealing with the internal wreckage wrought by the Fall. They were not simply cursed with thorny ground and pain in childbirth; they had to deal with their own ungodly impulses.

1. Genesis 4 follows up the story of the Fall with an account of the repercussions felt by the children of Adam. How do you account for Cain's reaction when the Lord rejects his offering?

2. What instruction does the Lord give Cain for dealing with his ungodly impulses?

3. Characterize Cain's response to the Lord when he is asked about Abel. How does his response change when the Lord convicts him of his sin?

The divine vending machine. During the days when the temple was standing in Jerusalem, people would bring offerings to the altar to find atonement for their sins. This was in keeping with the merciful provision of God in Leviticus 1–7. But out of a corrupt heart, people began to think of the sacrificial system like a divine vending machine: insert sheep, obtain atonement.

4. Examine the following Scriptures and answer this question: What kind of offering does God desire from sinful people?

- Psalm 50:7-15

- Isaiah 1:11-17

- Amos 5:21-24

- Micah 6:6-8

REFLECTIONS

Retraining our reflexes. Our patterns of slavery to sin do not fall away the moment we trust in Jesus. For many who experience a decisive conversion to Christ as adults, this comes as a startling discovery. After a few days or weeks of spiritual euphoria, an old sinful habit will assert itself with vigor or an old thought pattern of anger or lust will rear its ugly head. What are we to make of such old habits in a new man?

Perhaps we should say what's been said for years: Old habits die hard. A lead-footed driver will stomp on the brake pedal when he sees a patrol car, even after he has decided to drive the speed limit. This is the point Jeremiah made when he asked, "Can the Ethiopian change his skin or the leopard its spots? Neither can you do good who are accustomed to doing evil" (Jeremiah 13:23, NIV).

Yes, old habits die hard. And when it comes to sin, we're dealing with old, cherished habits. These die even harder.

For hundreds of years, Christians have believed that the consistent practice of spiritual disciplines will help ingrained, fleshly habits to die. In particular, the disciplines of silence, solitude, and fasting help a person break his unhealthy attachments to the world. These disciplines help us turn the tables on wrong impulses.

1. Which spiritual discipline—such as silence, solitude, or fasting—would you be willing to practice at regular intervals over the next month? Do you have a trusted friend who could join in praying for you and processing the experience with you? Start by writing out your plan below and feel free to seek the counsel of a respected Christian who can give you guidance about the how-tos.

Sickness, symptoms, and cure. When a person under extreme stress develops a headache, an aspirin will help dull the pain. It will not, however, cure the underlying problem. The headache is simply a symptom that presents itself, so that we (or others) can recognize the deeper problem.

Sinful behavior in ourselves or others—actions like overeating, gossiping, or harsh words—simply make a deeper problem manifest. The New Testament message of deliverance reaches to these deeper problems, to the heart of man. The gospel is not a short course on behavior modification, but "the power of God for salvation to everyone who believes" (Romans 1:16).

2. Describe the kind of church life that results when Christians give too much attention to curbing unacceptable behaviors within their fellowships. Which behaviors typically fall under scrutiny? Which ones get overlooked?

3. How does an overemphasis on behavior modification — that is, trying to change habits and actions — influence our ability to share the gospel with a lost world?

INTERSECTIONS

The heart of God for the heart of man. As the Israelites lived through the darkest days of bondage in Egypt, they cried out to God for deliverance. As Moses wrote, "Now it came about in the course of those many days that the king of Egypt died. And the sons of Israel sighed because of the bondage, and they cried out; and their cry for help because of their bondage rose up to God. So God heard their groaning; and God remembered His covenant with Abraham, Isaac, and Jacob. God saw the sons of Israel, and God took notice of them" (Exodus 2:23-25).

God longs to release from bondage those who cry out to Him for help. When you appeal to Him for the deliverance of your friends and family members who don't know Him, you are not wresting away from God something He doesn't want to give. The Lord longs to liberate those enslaved to sin.

1. What do the parables of Luke 15 tell you about God's desire to deliver "the tax collectors and the sinners [who came] near [Jesus] to listen to Him" (Luke 15:1)?

2. How will these stories influence the way you speak to God about the lost? How might they influence the way you speak to the lost about God?

Social progress and spiritual regress. Among the observations he made in solitude at Walden Pond, Henry David Thoreau commented, "While civilization has been improving our houses, it has not equally improved the men who are to inhabit them."[2]

We are surrounded by the promise of technology and advances in medicine. Our couches are more comfortable, and our cars run more efficiently. But the greatest problems are not in the world at all but in the hearts of those who inhabit it.

3. In what ways might the presence of modern conveniences actually hinder a person's spiritual growth? Consider the balance a Christian could strike between promoting the general welfare of his community but also advocating for the spiritual reformation of individuals in it.

LAY IT TO YOUR HEART

Meditate on the following passages and commit them to memory:

- Behold, the Lamb of God who takes away the sin of the world! (John 1:29)
- For He rescued us from the domain of darkness, and transferred us to the kingdom of His beloved Son, in whom we have redemption, the forgiveness of sins. (Colossians 1:13-14)
- He Himself bore our sins in His body on the cross, so that we might die to sin and live to righteousness; for by His wounds you were healed. (1 Peter 2:24)

RIGHTEOUSNESS WITHIN REACH

JESUS CAME TO CHANGE GOD'S PEOPLE, NOT GOD'S LAW ::

The great Spartan king Lycurgus developed a body of law so excellent that there seemed to be no room left for improvement. As the historian Plutarch wrote, the king looked "with joy and satisfaction at the greatness and beauty of his political structure [and] conceived the thought to make it immortal too, and, as far as human forecast could reach, to deliver it down unchangeable to posterity."[1]

Thus, he bound the Spartans to an oath not to alter the law until he had visited the oracle at Delphi and returned. The king consulted with the oracle and then starved himself to death without returning to Sparta, thereby ensuring the law should remain in effect always.

Let's take this account of Lycurgus and turn history into analogy. Suppose that this king's law really was perfect (though surely it was not). But let's also suppose that some fault could be found in the Spartan people —surely there were many—that rendered them unable to follow it. How could this situation be remedied? The people could not change themselves, nor could they change the law they had sworn on oath to obey.

Only one thing could deliver them from this impasse: the return of the king. So it is with the Law of the Moses and the coming of the Lord.

The Law that Moses received on Sinai was indeed perfect (Psalm 19:7), and the people of Israel had bound themselves to obey it (Exodus 19:7-8). However, it became obvious very quickly that the people of God did not have the wherewithal to obey the Law of God. In fact, the very first sin recorded after their oath was a transgression of the very first commandment God had given them! (Compare Exodus 20:1-3 with 32:1-8.)

The fault was not in the Law, but in the people. As Paul put it, "We know that the Law is spiritual, but I am of flesh" (Romans 7:14). Sinful men would need a radical solution if they were to obey the spiritual law. The King Himself would have to come to His people and change the Law . . . or change the people. Moses gave reason to hope that this day would come when he said: "The LORD your God will raise up for you a prophet like me from among you, from your countrymen, you shall listen to him. . . . The LORD said to me . . . 'I will raise up a prophet from among their countrymen like you, and I will put My words in his mouth, and he shall speak to them all that I command him. It shall come about that whoever will not listen to My words which he shall speak in My name, I Myself will require it of him'" (Deuteronomy 18:15-19).

Many in Jesus' day suspected He might be just this prophet foretold by Moses (see John 7:40-41). Whatever their perspective, Jesus' contemporaries could not fail to hear His straightforward words about the Mosaic Law. He claimed that He had come to fulfill it and set it aside as the basis upon which man would be declared righteous before God.

Still, many Jews in Jesus' day did not expect that the Messiah would do such a thing. Christians, if they believe anything at all, believe that He did.

Does this mean, then, that Christians dismiss the Law as irrelevant? In practice, many do. Few of them, however, do so because of what

Jesus and His apostles taught. Better for us to listen to Scripture than to hazard a guess.

A GUIDED EXPEDITION

Something more. To many of Jesus' contemporaries, He must have seemed like a renegade rabbi. He spoke with great authority and healed with great power, yet He avoided the spotlight and mingled with a questionable crowd. He certainly did not find a favorable reception among the religious authorities, whom He criticized publicly on many occasions.

So was Jesus a revolutionary or a reformer? Had He come to overthrow the system or to correct it? It is best to let Jesus answer these questions, as He does in Matthew 5:17-48.

1. Explain the contrast you see between "abolishing" and "fulfilling" the Law and Prophets.

2. The bottom line of the Law is that one must be righteous, as God is righteous, in order to experience life in God's kingdom. For people in Jesus' day, the Scribes and Pharisees were near—if not on—the pinnacle of righteousness. Describe the impact that Jesus' statement in Matthew 5:20 must have had on the common people who heard Him.

:: CERTIFICATE OF AUTHENTICITY

One of the greatest arguments for the authenticity of Scripture is its steadfast refusal to pare down Jesus' hard-to-understand teachings. He said, "Whoever keeps and teaches [the least of the commandments], he shall be called great in the kingdom of heaven" (Matthew 5:19). This is a teaching not easily squared with Paul's insistence that "Christ is the end of the law for righteousness to everyone who believes" (Romans 10:4). Nevertheless, the authors of Scripture, and the later compilers of the canon, did not feel the liberty to smooth over these difficulties. What Jesus Himself or Paul was authorized to reveal, the compilers had no authority to omit or amend. You can feel confident, if sometimes confused, that you are hearing what they actually said.

3. The rhetorical structure of Matthew 5:21-48 is hard to miss. Many sections begin, "You have heard that it was said [followed by an Old Testament citation] . . . but I say to you." Describe the overall impact this section of Scripture has on you.

4. Though Jesus insisted He did not come to abolish the Law, He hardly left it untouched in Matthew 5:21-48. Take note of the modifications Jesus made to the Law or the people's understanding of it by filling in the chart on the next page.

PASSAGE	THE LAW OF THE LORD SAYS . . .	THE LORD OF THE LAW INSISTS . . .
Matthew 5:21-24	You shall not commit murder and whoever commits murder shall be liable to the court (Genesis 9:6; Exodus 20:13; Numbers 35:12).	
Matthew 5:27-30	You shall not commit adultery (Exodus 20:14; Leviticus 20:10; Deuteronomy 22:22).	
Matthew 5:31-32	Whoever sends his wife away, let him give her a certificate of divorce (Deuteronomy 24:1-4).	
Matthew 5:33-37	You shall not make false vows, but shall fulfill your vows to the Lord (Leviticus 19:12; Numbers 30:1-16; Deuteronomy 23:21-23).	
Matthew 5:38-42	An eye for an eye, and a tooth for a tooth (Leviticus 24:17-22; Deuteronomy 19:21).	

PASSAGE	THE LAW OF THE LORD SAYS ...	THE LORD OF THE LAW INSISTS ...
Matthew 5:43-48	You shall love your neighbor and hate your enemy (Leviticus 19:17-18; Deuteronomy 23:3-6).	

5. How would you characterize the kinds of things Jesus taught about the Law? (Did He relax or raise the demands of righteousness? Did He render obedience more concrete or more abstract?)

6. In the Sermon on the Mount, Jesus demanded a righteousness that can come only from God. Describe some definite way you have experienced divine grace to live free from anger (Matthew 5:22) or lust (5:28). In what discoverable ways have you been strengthened to remain faithful to your spouse (5:32) or to love those who oppose you (5:44)?

Breaking the barrier. In the early years of the church, few Gentiles had heard and embraced the gospel of Jesus Christ. Almost all the early Christians were Jews. In fact, the Christian church was still identified as a sect of Judaism at the close of the New Testament era (see Acts 24:5,14;

28:22). As the gospel message began to spread outward to the Gentile world, however, the predominantly Jewish church had to answer a tough question: Could Gentiles be saved without obeying the Mosaic Law? This question was taken up during the council of Jerusalem, recorded in Acts 15:1-33.

7. Describe the specific circumstances that prompted this meeting and the prominent figures who took part in it.

8. Summarize the contribution that each of the following made to the discussion and debate at the council:

■ Paul and Barnabas (15:4,12)

■ Some of the Pharisees who had believed (15:5)

■ Peter (15:7-11)

■ James (15:13-21)

9. Describe what steps the council took to communicate their decision to the Gentile Christians at Antioch. Why do you suppose they communicated their message in this way?

::CONVERSION NOT ADVISED

In history, Jews have not been known as ardent evangelists, seeking to win converts among the Gentiles. Some Jewish rabbis would actually attempt to dissuade a prospective Gentile from converting to Judaism, for a Gentile obligates himself to obey the whole Law (613 commandments), not just the seven laws given to Noah upon conversion.[2] Against this backdrop, you can see why the council of Jerusalem represented a tectonic shift in evangelism. With one mind, the Jews who comprised the Christian church were encouraging Gentiles to convert to the faith of Abraham.

10. From the chronological marker found in Galatians 2:1, how long did it take the church to determine that Gentiles could be full believers in Christ without taking on the yoke of the Mosaic Law?

::FREE TO BE OBSERVANT

The same gospel that sets a Jew free from observing the Mosaic Law also sets him free to obey it if he so chooses. It is a rare Gentile who would willingly adopt the dietary laws of Leviticus. A Jewish Christian, however, might not wish to live without them. The gospel does not command a Gentile to keep a kosher diet or a Jew to forsake it. The gospel simply commands all men to seek their righteousness in Jesus alone without seeking to establish their own through obedience to commandments (see Romans 10:3). About matters of conscience, preference, and custom, there is liberty . . . even liberty to obey the Law. For New Testament examples of this principle in practice, see Acts 18:18 and 21:17-26.

11. The decision of the council at Jerusalem was hammered out in debate with Christian Pharisees, a group known for intense religious devotion and intellectual rigor. Acts 15:5 records these

Pharisees' position. Put yourself in their shoes and consider how they might have supported their contention:

- On logical grounds

- On biblical grounds

- On social grounds

12. Can you envision what life as a Christian would look like if the Pharisees had carried the day at the council of Jerusalem? Think through an encounter with a friend where you share the "good news" about salvation through Jesus' death along with the necessity of getting circumcised and the responsibility to keep the 613 laws of Moses.

Salvation apart from the Law. Throughout the New Testament era, the apostles often restated clearly how man related to God through faith in Christ apart from the Old Testament Law. Paul addressed this issue in Romans 3:21-31.

13. According to Paul, how does a person gain right standing before God?

14. What role do the Law and prophets play in leading a person to salvation?

15. Though many observant Jews would claim that Christians violate the Mosaic Law, Paul concludes this passage by saying, "Do we then nullify the Law through faith? May it never be! On the contrary, we establish [uphold] the Law" (Romans 3:31). How would you explain Paul's logic to a friend who is confused by such a statement?

:: BRINGING US ALL TOGETHER

In Romans 1, Paul addressed the false beliefs and sinful behavior that led the Gentile world into judgment. In Romans 2, he turned his pen to a hypothetical Jewish onlooker and said, in effect, "Though you have the Law, you are no better off than a pagan since you don't keep it." Then in Romans 3, Paul brought both audiences together to assure us all that the only thing as universal as human sin (3:9-10) is the salvation Jesus offers (3:29-30).

AN OLD TESTAMENT EXCURSION

Reverence for the Law. While the New Testament is unanimous in teaching that salvation comes by God's grace through faith in Jesus alone, it also affirms that "the Law is holy, and the commandment is holy and righteous and good" (Romans 7:12). What a contrast this forms with the popular sentiment among most Christians that the Law is holy . . . and confusing and scary!

If we intend to think biblically about the Law, we will need to find a biblical appreciation of it, and there is no better place to start than in the poetry of Psalm 19.

1. What connections do you observe between the testimony of the heavens (Psalm 19:1-6) and the testimony of the Law (19:7-11) in this poem?

2. With what words does the psalmist characterize the excellence of the Law?

3. What influence does the Law exercise on the person who embraces it?

From arithmetic to calculus. Many people today consider the Old Testament Law obscure because they plunge into its complexities without an elementary understanding of its basics, like one who tries to master calculus without finishing a course on arithmetic. Jesus Himself taught us the "arithmetic" of the Law when He said that all of it can be summed up under the two headings of loving God and loving your neighbor (see Mark 12:28-34).

4. Read Leviticus 19 and offer five examples under each heading.

COMMANDS THAT INDICATE HOW WE CAN LOVE GOD WITH ALL OUR HEART, MIND, SOUL, AND STRENGTH	COMMANDS THAT INDICATE HOW WE CAN LOVE OUR NEIGHBORS AS OURSELVES	COMMANDS THAT DON'T FIT NEATLY UNDER EITHER HEADING

REFLECTIONS

Our tendency toward legalism. God never intended His Law to be used by men (or against them) as a checklist to determine who has done enough to please God. However, that is how many people in religious circles have used the Mosaic Law, or some pared-down version of it. It seems easier for us to obey rules than to live in relationship with a God who is as mysterious as the wind and holy as fire, yet near as the air we breathe and dear enough to be called "Father."

1. Why do you suppose that we tend to use the Law as a checklist for measuring our performance for God?

2. What effect does this kind of religious devotion have in our own hearts? How does it influence the way we relate to others?

What's the Law for? Consider the straightforward question, "What's a dictionary for?" Most people wouldn't have to think too long to respond, "To look up the meaning of words." However, most of us also use the dictionary for other purposes, as well. To determine the pronunciation of a word or discover its historical origins . . . or even to settle a dispute in a game of Scrabble! In short, a book may have more than one use.

The same can be said of the Law of Moses. Most people would say that the Law was given to show the best way to live. However, the New Testament offers a fuller, more nuanced, answer than this.

3. Look at the following passages and summarize why the Law of Moses was given.

PASSAGE	WHY WAS THE LAW GIVEN?
Romans 3:19-20	
Romans 5:20	
Romans 7:7	
Galatians 3:19	
Galatians 3:23-24	

INTERSECTIONS

The relevance of the Old Testament Law. Christians who affirm the authority and relevance of the whole Bible are often asked to explain how the Old Testament laws prescribing capital punishment are to be applied today. "Should a homosexual be stoned to death? Or an adulterer? Or a teen who has premarital sex?" These and many other vexing issues are presented in the Old Testament. How would you answer such questions?

Removing the roadblocks. At the council of Jerusalem, James summarized the church's desire that Gentiles not be troubled or burdened about Jewish laws requiring circumcision. The church did not want to shut the door of salvation on the Gentiles by putting up unnecessary social barriers.

What are some barriers modern Christians have put up (or not taken down) that impede nonbelievers from finding salvation in Christ? Although you may be aware of some of these, your nonbelieving friends could tell you of many others if asked. Interview one or two nonbelieving friends or family members and ask how they think they would have to change to become a part of your Christian fellowship. Ask them what they would change about the church to make it more receptive to all people.

You need not agree with all their answers, but neither should you attempt to convince your friend or family member that he is wrong. You simply want to gather information in this interview, not offer it. Do not seek to defend any of your practices or dispel any of the person's misunderstandings about the church, unless he opens the door for you to talk. Just listen and learn. Perhaps you will discover how you and your church can minimize the "trouble [of] those who are turning to God from among the Gentiles" (Acts 15:19).

LAY IT TO YOUR HEART

Meditate on the following passages and commit them to memory:

- 'You shall love the Lord your God with all your heart, and with all your soul, and with all your mind.' This is the great and foremost commandment. The second is like it, 'You shall love your neighbor as yourself.' On these two commandments depend the whole Law and the Prophets. (Matthew 22:37-40)
- But now apart from the Law the righteousness of God has been manifested, being witnessed by the Law and the Prophets, even the righteousness of God through faith in Jesus Christ for all those who believe. (Romans 3:21-22)
- For Christ is the end of the law for righteousness to everyone who believes. (Romans 10:4)

WHERE ON EARTH DOES GOD LIVE?

THE LORD'S DWELLING AMONG US ::

The temple in Jerusalem stood at a high point in the city, such that everyone could look up and see the place where God dwelt. Of course, no one believed that God was actually contained in a twelve-by-twelve-foot room. Solomon had set this straight from the beginning: "But will God indeed dwell with mankind on the earth? Behold, heaven and the highest heaven cannot contain You; how much less this house which I have built" (2 Chronicles 6:18). Yet somehow, this place was unique. God Himself had commanded that the Israelites build Him a temple, a "house" or home He had called it (1 Chronicles 22:9-10). Surely, it was a mystery how the God who filled the heavens and the earth could also dwell between the hammered-gold wings of angels in a sacred room in the temple. Yet it was so.

What was it all about? Why did God excite this tension between the loftiness of His being and the earthiness of His home?

You might say that God was laying the foundations for the gospel while Solomon was laying the foundations of the temple. The temple, and the mobile tabernacle that preceded it, introduced into the Jewish mindset inescapable truths about God and His relation to man.

The temple told Jews, and indeed the whole world, that God wanted to dwell in the midst of His people (see 2 Chronicles 6:32-33). He was not the god of the idol-worshipers—a distant deity who thundered at man across a cosmic gulf while they bowed before a mute statue. (When God thundered, He thundered from Zion, the temple mount!) Nor was He the god of the pantheistic philosophers—a passionless, pervasive life force that made no demands and offered no promises.

God declared Himself to be a personality, a presence. Not a mere force but a Father—a heavenly Father who dwells with His children on earth. The temple stood as a brick-and-mortar testimony that Almighty God could somehow localize Himself among men without surrendering any of His power and might. That was one inescapable message of the temple.

How great an irony, then, that the temple should also tell men that the God who desired to dwell among them could not be approached by sinners! God would be in our midst, but we could not be in His unless He wiped our sins away.

Now, by reading the story backward through Jesus, we can see clearly how the temple's presence in Jerusalem prepared humanity to receive the Son of God. We knew that God sought to dwell among people, but we knew that He would have to purify us so we could dwell with Him.

Who could have seen that the Father would do both these things by sending His only Son, who stood up one day and announced, "Something greater than the temple is here" (Matthew 12:6)? And who could have anticipated that the same God who "became flesh, and dwelt among us" (John 1:14) would also come to dwell within us? When the Christian church was founded, He did not shift His residence from Jerusalem to Rome. He took up residence by His Spirit in His people. Our bodies became His temple, and our churches became His body.

A GUIDED EXPEDITION

Destroy this temple. After turning water to wine in Cana of Galilee, Jesus traveled to His hometown for a few days and then on to the capital city of Jerusalem to celebrate the Passover. As He entered the precincts of the temple, the Son of God was approaching the one place on earth where the Father dwelt in manifest form (see Matthew 23:21). Contrary to what you might expect, however, this was not a happy homecoming. As we discover in John 2:13-22, Jesus entered the temple incensed at the corruption in His Father's house.

1. Describe the state of affairs Jesus observed when He entered the temple.

:: THE CASH COW

Even before the Jewish people inherited a homeland, they were instructed to come before the Lord "at the place which the LORD your God will choose from all your tribes, to establish His name there for His dwelling. . . . There you shall bring your burnt offerings, your sacrifices, your tithes, the contribution of your hand, your votive offerings, your freewill offerings, and the firstborn of your herd and of your flock" (Deuteronomy 12:5-6). But how was a person to bring the sheep and oxen for his offerings if he lived at a great distance from Jerusalem? The Law included this proviso: "If the distance is so great for you that you are not able to bring the tithe, since the place where the LORD your God chooses to set His name is too far away from you when the LORD your God blesses you, then you shall exchange it for money, and bind the money in your hand and go to the place which the LORD your God chooses. [Once there,] You may spend the money for whatever your heart desires: for oxen, or sheep, or wine, or strong drink, or whatever your heart desires; and there you shall eat in the presence of the

Lᴏʀᴅ your God and rejoice, you and your household" (Deuteronomy 14:24-26).

The moneychangers and retailers whom Jesus kicked out of the temple were the agents authorized to sell the ritually clean animals and wine referred to in Deuteronomy 14. We may infer from Jesus' actions against them that these retailers were more concerned with fleecing the faithful than facilitating temple worship.

2. What actions and accusations did Jesus bring against the merchants in the temple and the religious leaders who authorized them to be there?

3. Indignant with Jesus' behavior, the Jews (i.e., the religious leaders) demanded that Jesus show them some sign to verify His authority to oppose the temple establishment. What sign did Jesus tell them to look for?

4. How did the religious leaders respond to Jesus? What about His disciples (at the time)?

5. When Jesus was raised from the dead, John asserted that the disciples remembered what He had declared at the temple. What do you suppose they "believed [about] the Scripture and the word which Jesus had spoken" (John 2:22)?

:: ANYTHING YOU SAY CAN BE USED AGAINST YOU

Jesus said, "Destroy this temple, and in three days I will raise it up" (John 2:19). Jesus' words would turn up again at the end of His earthly ministry when He stood before the Jewish council that was seeking formal testimony against Him. After running through several inconsistent witnesses, two came forward and said, "This man stated, 'I am able to destroy the temple of God and to rebuild it in three days'" (Matthew 26:60-61). Given the atmosphere of political tension, any talk of treason was just the kind of testimony the council needed to condemn Jesus. Talking about destroying the temple in Jesus' day registered like a conversation might in ours about "blowing up the White House." Thus, Jesus' early words about His death and resurrection were the very words that sealed His death sentence and led to His crucifixion.

6. It was not a happy day when Jesus walked into the midst of sinners in the temple. What about you? Do you want the Lord to draw near to you? That probably depends. If a child is coloring on the bedroom walls with a crayon, she doesn't want her father to walk in. However, if she has been caught, she doesn't want her father to turn away from her in anger. God has come near to you with a full knowledge of your sin and a full offer of forgiveness. In what ways is God's response to our wrongdoing and failures

different from the response of our earthly authority figures (parents, bosses, teachers, and so on)?

Our bodies are temples. God was born in the likeness of a man that man might be reborn in the likeness of God. Jesus became a man so that man could become like Him. But just how far does this likeness extend? Does it involve more than just a spiritual union with God in Christ, or might our bodies be involved in the redemption, too?

Though the timid may blush at this suggestion, there is no better way to tackle questions like these than to consider human sexuality. That is precisely what Paul did in 1 Corinthians 6:12-20 as he helped the church think theologically and practically about our bodies. Paul cited two proverbs in use among the Corinthians that boil down their attitude toward the body.

7. What do you suppose these sayings mean?

■ All things are lawful for me. (1 Corinthians 6:12)

■ Food is for the stomach and the stomach is for food. (6:13)

8. What kind of excesses could you predict arising from those beliefs about the body if they were left unmodified by any others?

9. Paul offers a theological check—you might even say theological complexity—to the Corinthians' oversimplified beliefs about their bodies. Identify every instance of the words *body* or *bodies* in 1 Corinthians 6:13-20, and write out five statements that Paul would have Christians understand about their bodies.

10. Our bodies are not ours to misuse, for they belong to God. He means for us to bring Him glory with our bodies, just as we do our hearts and minds. That is, He wants us to bring our whole person—soul, mind, and body—under the influence of His divine grace and command. Describe the struggles you have faced in bringing your body into submission to God's will. (These sins generally fall under the categories of neglect or indulgence.) How does the biblical declaration that your body is God's temple bolster your courage to face these areas of sin?

::FORGETTING WHAT LIES BEHIND

We should not allow the experience of past failures to dim or destroy our hopes that we can live fully submitted to God with our bodies. Past failures only have the power to tell us where we have gone wrong; they have no authority to tell us we cannot go right. Nor should any Christian say, "I have gone too far down this road of neglect or indulgence to turn back now. If I could turn back the clock a few years, maybe. But not now."

God asks no one to be faithful with yesterday's opportunities, only to be stewards of today's choices. The only proper response to previous failures is confession and repentance. Today, we may take the steps necessary sincerely to intend and intentionally to pursue a life of bodily holiness. God will give us grace for today and perfect our intention into eternity!

The "body" is the temple of God. What do you get when you combine one believer, whose body is a temple of God, with another, whose body is also God's temple? From God's perspective you get one body and one temple, comprised of the two. And if you add another two or three or twenty believers, the total still comes to one body — the body of Christ on earth. Though made up of different parts, our union in Christ means we are one entity. That is the "new math" Paul made clear in Ephesians 2:11-22.

11. Consider Paul's metaphors in this passage, and fill in the following sentences with words you find most appropriate to his meaning:

   ■ In Christ we are not simply an association of inspired individuals; rather, we are one _____ (Ephesians 2:15-16).
   ■ In Christ we are not simply a collection of cordial strangers; rather, we are one _____ (2:19).
   ■ In Christ, we do not lie about as a random collection of stones; rather, we are one _____ (2:21-22).

12. This passage says that Jesus is the cornerstone of the church, while the teaching of the apostles and prophets forms its foundation. Expand on the implications of this metaphor by considering what role a cornerstone and foundation play in building a house . . . or a temple.

13. Ancient temples exist in many parts of the world. To us, they are relics and ruins; however, in their day, these temples were not tourist destinations but places of service and worship. What kind of service and worship should God's temple—the church—be rendering today? What sorts of negative influences could render us a ruin or relic in the future?

AN OLD TESTAMENT EXCURSION

Temple with a capital "T." When Jesus and the apostles refer to the temple in the New Testament, they are referring to one definite building complex that stood on a hill in Jerusalem. Looking at this building's history and significance in the Old Testament will help us understand the New Testament references to it.

:: TEMPLE WORSHIP REIGNITED

By the middle of the second century BC, Jews were being heavily pressured to accommodate their religious and cultural practices to the traditions of Greece. Antiochus Epiphanes, the tyrant of the Seleucid Empire, was determined to assimilate Jews into Hellenistic culture at all costs. To sever them from their religious heritage, "the king sent letters by messengers to Jerusalem and the towns of Judah; he directed them to follow customs strange to the land, to forbid burnt offerings and sacrifices and drink offerings in the sanctuary . . . to defile the sanctuary and the priests, to build altars and sacred precincts and shrines for idols, to sacrifice swine and other unclean animals" (1 Maccabees 1:44-47).

Such aggression against the temple and the Law ignited a revolt led by the five sons of a man named Matthias, a revolt that eventually led to full Jewish independence. The story of this revolt may be read in the deuterocanonical books of 1 and 2 Maccabees. The Jewish celebration of Hanukkah commemorates the restoration of temple worship after the demise of Antiochus.

1. In what ways do the following Old Testament passages enrich your understanding of the New Testament concepts we have studied?

OLD TESTAMENT CONCEPT AND PASSAGE	NEW TESTAMENT CONCEPT: JESUS CALLED HIS OWN BODY THE TEMPLE	NEW TESTAMENT CONCEPT: OUR BODIES ARE THE TEMPLE OF THE HOLY SPIRIT	NEW TESTAMENT CONCEPT: THE CHURCH IS THE TEMPLE OF GOD
The glory of God filled the temple: 1 Kings 8:6-11 (compare with Exodus 40:34-38)			
The glory of God departed from the temple: Ezekiel 10:3-4,18-19; 11:22-23			
God desired His ruined temple to be rebuilt and promised to fill it again: Haggai 1:1-11; 2:6-9			

REFLECTIONS

With all your heart, mind, and strength. When a man asks for a woman's hand in marriage, he generally gets the rest of her at the altar as well. When you gave your heart to Jesus, did you know He would expect your body too?

God will not rest content with our hearts and minds only. Nor should we, for we would be failing to heed the foremost commandment: "Hear, O Israel! The LORD is our God, the LORD is one! You shall love the LORD your God with all your heart and with all your soul and with all your might" (Deuteronomy 6:4-5; see also Mark 12:29-30). We cannot live out a disembodied Christian spirituality. There is no such thing.

1. Explore some ways you can "present your bodies a living and holy sacrifice, acceptable to God" (Romans 12:1). Can you adjust your habits of eating, exercise, or sleep to present your body as a holy sacrifice to God? What habits has God led you to take up or to give up as He brings your body into conformity with His will?

2. How have your struggles with bodily sin undermined your resolve to love God with all your heart and mind? How do your struggles with sin undermine your willingness and resolve to seek again to honor God with your body?

More than one way to profane a temple. In Scripture, God makes it plain that He will personally oppose anyone who destroys or profanes His temple. The Old Testament illustrates this point vividly in the account of Belshazzar's fate (Daniel 5). His kingdom was stripped from him by the Medo-Persian army on the very night he profaned the sacred vessels from the Jewish temple.

Paul put the point bluntly in 1 Corinthians 3:16-17: "Do you not know that you are a temple of God and that the Spirit of God dwells in you? If any man destroys the temple of God, God will destroy him, for the temple of God is holy, and that is what you are."

We would be well-advised to ask, then, how a person might destroy or profane the temple. Jeremiah 7:1-11 provides one of the most striking answers.

3. The Jews in Jeremiah's day felt false security because the temple was in their midst. What sins did the Lord reprove them for, though they regularly entered the temple to worship?

4. In what ways should we in the church today be advised by this warning from the past?

INTERSECTIONS

All in the family. From Ephesians, we learn that Jesus combines diverse and different people in His body. Before He came and "broke down the barrier of the dividing wall" (Ephesians 2:14), Jews and Gentiles would not even sit at the same table to eat together. After He came, Jesus declared them "one new man." As Paul put it elsewhere, "There is no distinction between Greek and Jew, circumcised and uncircumcised, barbarian, Scythian, slave and freeman, but Christ is all, and in all" (Colossians 3:11).

In short, Jesus didn't come to make peace between man and God only, but also between one human and another. In practice, however, the church seems to belie this claim.

1. How would you assess the unity between Christians in your community with diverse ethnic backgrounds?

2. What signal do you think we send the world when Christians of different ethnicity are largely segregated in their worship and fellowship?

3. How might the church's witness be strengthened if Christians chose to live in unity with others of different ethnic groups? What kind of practical steps could you take toward this end?

Obsessing about the body. All the worst Christian heresies and many non-Christian religions knock the relation of the body and the soul out of balance. When the soul is reckoned to be the only thing that really matters, the body will be treated as an irrelevancy or a hindrance to real spiritual progress.

4. How does a vibrant Christian doctrine of body and soul help maintain the balance?

5. What difference does the doctrine of the resurrection—that God "will transform the body of our humble state into conformity with the body of His glory" (Philippians 3:21)—make as we think about our bodies and souls on earth?

6. Have you observed any imbalance in the way our culture views the body or the soul? If so, where does the imbalance originate, and where is it leading?

LAY IT TO YOUR HEART

Meditate on the following passages and commit them to memory:

- My dwelling place also will be with them; and I will be their God, and they will be My people. And the nations will know that I am the LORD who sanctifies Israel, when My sanctuary is in their midst forever. (Ezekiel 37:27-28)
- And the Word became flesh, and dwelt among us, and we saw His glory, glory as of the only begotten from the Father, full of grace and truth. (John 1:14)
- Do you not know that your body is a temple of the Holy Spirit who is in you, whom you have from God, and that you are not your own? (1 Corinthians 6:19)

A MAN CALLED MESSIAH

REVELATION, REDEMPTION, AND A RENEGADE RABBI ::

The first lines of the New Testament begin: "The record of the genealogy of Jesus the Messiah, the son of David, the son of Abraham" (Matthew 1:1). Those who begin reading the Bible at this point may justly conclude that the advent of Jesus formed the pivotal point of all history and theology.

But limiting your Bible reading to the New Testament leaves you wholly unaware that the Messiah did not leap onto the stage of human history unannounced. Far from it. Jewish expectations about the Messiah were as old as Eden. There, God had told Adam and Eve that one of their offspring would bruise the Serpent's head.

From Eden onward, God announced time and again His intention to send a Savior to redeem Israel from its sin and to shine light upon the nations dwelling in darkness. The fact of the Messiah's coming was not in doubt to anyone who read the Scriptures. The means of His coming was less clear. And the timing of His arrival was impossible to predict.

Ample prophecies pointed an entire generation to Jesus, but these were, after all, only pointers, not portraits. God left enough room in His predictions for men to believe in Jesus . . . or not.

The prophecies of the Old Testament were like the parables that Jesus Himself uttered. Some people understood them and believed. Others wanted to understand, so they sought out Jesus for an explanation. Still others were mystified and concluded that Jesus was crazy or even demon-possessed.

So it was also with the signs Jesus performed on earth. Those whose hearts were inclined toward God saw the signs pointing toward the heaven-born Son of the Father. Those whose hearts were hardened saw the same signs and believed these indicated Jesus' hellish allegiance with the prince of demons.

The prophecies, parables, and signs all beckon a man to believe. They do not, however, *compel* a man to believe, for nothing can compel belief. Trust does not answer to compulsion, but to truth . . . and probably love.

Are the Old Testament prophecies true? Do they indeed point toward Jesus, announcing Him to be the long-expected Savior?

That is precisely what the New Testament writers insisted. They told about Jesus' mysterious birth by quoting passages from the Old Testament. They insisted that His sufferings line up with the predictions of the ancient prophets. They even said that His resurrection and Second Coming are certain, because the Scriptures of the Old Testament declare that both must happen.

This confidence in the Old Testament testimony is more striking when we realize that the men who confessed it so plainly didn't or couldn't or wouldn't believe it when Jesus said so! The New Testament writers were humble enough to say they misunderstood Jesus up until the day He was crucified, and even some days after He was raised again.

Eventually, however, these men understood and announced the plain truth about Jesus: "Let all the house of Israel know for certain that God has made Him both Lord and Christ [Messiah] — this Jesus whom you crucified" (Acts 2:36). What they arrived at after years of confusion, we may read with clarity in a sitting, for they wrote the New Testament "that [we] may believe that Jesus is the Christ, the Son of God; and that believing [we] may have life in His name" (John 20:31).

:: A PARADE OF PROPHETS AND PROPHECIES

Blaise Pascal pointed out how significant it is that so many different people, over so many different centuries, all consistently foretold the Messiah's coming: "If one man alone had made a book of predictions about Jesus Christ, as to the time and the manner, and Jesus Christ had come in conformity to these prophecies, this fact would have infinite weight. But there is much more here. Here is a succession of men during four thousand years, who, consequently and without variation, come, one after another, to foretell this same event. . . . This is far more important."[1]

A GUIDED EXPEDITION

The Messiah in a manger. Many nonreligious people know the account of Jesus' birth, since we commemorate it at Christmas with nativity scenes and reenactments. Certainly, most Christians could rehearse the story by heart. Yet our familiarity with Jesus' birth can actually keep us from seeing the astonishing scandal of it all! After all, the Messiah was born to a poor family, to an unwed mother, and spent His early years on the run from the authorities.

We can recover the startling realities surrounding His birth only when we turn away from the holiday decorations and read Scriptures, such as Matthew 1–2.

1. Matthew begins by presenting an account of Jesus' genealogy — hardly a gripping way to begin a narrative. What purpose do these details serve?

::NOT A PERFECT PEDIGREE

In addition to Mary, Matthew mentions four women in Jesus' genealogy — all of whom share a common trait. They don't seem to belong on the family tree of the Jewish Messiah! Rahab was a Canaanite, Ruth was a Moabite, and Bathsheba was likely a Hittite. This means their Jewish husbands broke the Law by marrying them (see Deuteronomy 7:1-4). Three of them — Tamar, Rahab, and Bathsheba — were mixed up in sexual sin: incest, prostitution, and adultery, respectively. The genealogy of Jesus was certainly not offered to point out His spotless family pedigree. Rather, His earthly family was comprised of the same kind of people who now make up His spiritual family: people with a forgiven past and a present faith.

2. Matthew anchored Jesus' genealogy to three key Old Testament figures or events (see 1:17). Describe the significance of each in the salvation history of Israel.

   - Abraham

   - David

   - The deportation to Babylon

3. Mary and Joseph did not arbitrarily land on the name Jesus for their new baby (the Hebrew would have been closer to our Joshua). God Himself revealed the name to them, indicating that Jesus would fulfill what destiny?

4. While Matthew began with a survey of Jesus' Jewish lineage, he makes it clear that Mary conceived Him by the Holy Spirit before she had ever slept with Joseph. According to 1:22-23, why did Jesus' birth happen in this miraculous fashion? Can you suggest any other reasons the Messiah came into the world this way?

5. Summarize your impressions of 2:1-12: What significance do you discern in the magi's coming to pay homage to Jesus? How do you suppose these kings knew the significance of the star that led them to Jesus? How did the chief priests and scribes know where to direct them?

6. In what ways did practical necessity and prophetic destiny combine in the flight of Jesus' family to Egypt? How about in regard to their return to Galilee instead of Nazareth?

7. Jesus was born into trouble so we could see that divine salvation is often born out of it. Desperate circumstances give God ample opportunity to display His divine providence. Describe a recent time of hardship where it was difficult to see how God

could bring about His good purposes for you and for others. How might meditation on the circumstances of Jesus' birth provide an anchor for your faith and hope in God's providence?

The Messiah's entourage. Though Jesus was regarded as a rabbi, He kept company with an unconventional crowd. Not only did He think it appropriate to share meals with "tax collectors and sinners" (Mark 2:15), He selected as disciples men of diverse professions and dispositions "that they would be with Him and that He could send them out to preach, and to have authority to cast out the demons" (3:14-15). They were hardly the religious or intellectual elite; however, they were men who loved Jesus and listened to Him . . . most of the time.

We learn in Luke 24:13-35, however, that Jesus' disciples had a hard time embracing all His words. In spite of what He had done to prepare them for it, Jesus' disciples were blindsided by His arrest and execution.

8. Judging from Luke 24:13-24, how would you describe the mood of the disciples Jesus met on the road to Emmaus after His resurrection?

:: SIGN-DEAF

We are tempted to think that miraculous signs provide the most compelling evidence of God's existence and will. Jesus did not share this point of view. In fact, He rebuked it by telling the story of a rich man who died and went to hell about the same time that a poor man died and went to heaven. Out of his torment, the rich man implored Abraham to send the poor man back from the dead to warn his brothers about hell. Abraham replied, "They have Moses and the Prophets; let them hear them" (Luke 16:29). When the rich man protested that his brothers were deaf to the Scriptures but would listen if someone came back from the dead, Abraham responded, "If they do not listen to Moses and the Prophets, they will not be persuaded even if someone rises from the dead" (16:31). From Jesus' own teaching, we may conclude that the greatest proofs of His divinity are to be found in the written Word.

9. Cleopas and the other disciple confess that their hopes had been dashed when Jesus was crucified. What do you suppose they had been hoping for from Jesus? How had His destiny ruined their expectations?

10. What means did Jesus adopt to realign His disciples' thinking? Why do you suppose He chose this route of instruction rather than unveiling Himself to them visibly?

11. Have you ever asked the question, or even cried out, "If only God would come down and speak to me!"? What if He already has? Or what if, as the disciples found, He came but kept you from perceiving who He was? Is it not quite probable that He would take you right back to the Scriptures that you have been reading or listening to all along? Think through the times in your life when you have most consistently and thoroughly immersed yourself in the teachings of the Bible. What were the factors that helped you strike and stay on that course?

The Messiah's ministry. If the message of Jesus' humble birth was hard for some to swallow, harder still was the message of His humiliating death. Wasn't the Messiah supposed to crush wickedness on earth? This Messiah appeared to be crushed by it. How in the world did His disciples ever work up the nerve to proclaim Him Messiah who was born a peasant and died like a criminal? Listen to Peter as he explains this to a large crowd in Acts 3:11-26. The crowd had gathered around Peter and John because they had just healed a beggar whom regular temple-goers knew to be lame.

12. Where did Peter claim his healing power had come from?

13. Examine the different words or expressions Peter uses to identify Jesus throughout this passage. How does each one cast a different light on the character or accomplishments of Jesus?

14. What accusation does Peter bring against the crowd for the way they responded to Jesus? On the other hand, what allowance does he make for their treachery (see Acts 3:17-18)?

15. Peter claims that the disciples were witnesses of the Resurrection. However, he also claims that the prophets foretold the things that would happen to Jesus and how the people should respond to Him. What prophecies does Peter point the temple crowd to, and how does he urge them to respond?

::THE CRUX OF CHRISTIAN BELIEF

Although Jewish sages held different views about the manner of the Messiah's advent, they all agreed on one thing: When He came, He would liberate Israel from the yoke of Gentile oppression. Jesus' own disciples were incapable of conceiving a messianic ministry otherwise (Matthew 20:20-28; Luke 24:19-21; Acts 1:6). How challenging it must have been for them to begin a ministry of evangelization among their Jewish contemporaries with a message about the Messiah who had been executed! Indeed, this proved to be a stumbling block to the Jews (see 1 Corinthians 1:23; Galatians 5:11).

16. List three lessons you learn from Acts 3 about proclaiming the gospel to those who have rejected Jesus. Take into consideration the content of Peter's message, the situation in which the opportunity arose, and the audience he spoke to.

The Messiah in majesty. Though Jesus brought us salvation through humiliation, He will come again to earth someday in incomparable might and majesty. He began the work of redemption in swaddling cloths; He will end it in raiment that defies description. All the messianic longings for a righteous Ruler who will put an end to wickedness will be fulfilled at His Second Coming. Even if we missed the message about His suffering in the Old Testament prophecies, it would be hard to miss the descriptions of His exaltation in passages like Revelation 1.

17. List all the people who had a hand in bringing the book of Revelation to light, according to Revelation 1:1-3.

18. Which words or phrases describing Jesus create the greatest impression on you?

19. From the statement in 1:5-6 and the image of 1:12-20, describe the relationship that Jesus maintains with His people, His church.

20. When John declares that Jesus "is coming with the clouds" (Revelation 1:7), he is making a direct connection to the prophetic vision of Daniel 7. In this vision, Daniel saw earthly kingdoms, "beasts," that ruled for a time but ultimately stood in judgment before God's divine court at the end of the age. What connections do you observe between Daniel's vision in Daniel 7:9-18 and John's vision in Revelation 1?

21. Many people avoid Bible prophecies because parts seem obscure to them. Yet our reluctance to read and understand these parts of the Bible might actually undermine our faith, for the New Testament writers seem to have held the view of Pascal, who said that "the prophecies are the strongest proof of Jesus Christ."[2] What steps could you take to acquaint yourself with the key prophecies about Jesus' birth? And His Second Coming? How might such a familiarity with prophecy aid you in presenting the gospel to nonbelievers?

AN OLD TESTAMENT EXCURSION

Feel the tension. Jesus' disciples were positively confounded by all His talk about suffering. Their expectations about the Messiah were like a round hole and His pronouncements about His death—no matter how direct—were like a square peg. Consider this interaction from Luke 18:31-34:

> Then He [Jesus] took the twelve aside and said to them, "Behold, we are going up to Jerusalem, and all things which are written through the prophets about the Son of Man will be accomplished. For He will be handed over to the Gentiles, and will be mocked and mistreated and spit upon, and after they have scourged Him, they will kill Him; and the third day He will rise again."
>
> But the disciples understood none of these things, and the meaning of this statement was hidden from them, and they did not comprehend the things that were said.

Jesus' disciples did not have room in their mental framework for the suffering and death of Jesus, because they embraced only half the messianic predictions of the Old Testament—the half that spoke about the Messiah's Second Coming in power. They missed, or misinterpreted, the other half of the prophecies that spoke about His humiliation as a man.

1. We should not be too hard on the disciples, however, for who could have envisioned the Old Testament prophecies about the Messiah coming together in one man? To get a feel for the tension God intended, compare and contrast the two columns below.

FIRST, READ ALL THE PASSAGES IN THIS COLUMN TOGETHER AND ANSWER THE QUESTION BELOW	NEXT, READ ALL THE PASSAGES IN THIS COLUMN TOGETHER AND ANSWER THE QUESTION BELOW
Psalm 2 Isaiah 43:1-7 Daniel 9:25-26	Psalm 22 Isaiah 53:1-12 Jeremiah 33:14-18
Describe the kind of Messiah you would expect if you embraced only the passages in this column.	Describe kind of Messiah you would expect if you embraced only the passages in this column.

REFLECTIONS

Walking in the way of the Messiah. Most of Jesus' contemporaries rejected Him as the Messiah because He deliberately chose a life of self-denial, service, and suffering. Though it is sometimes hard for us to accept, that is the way He will ask us to walk, too. "If anyone wishes to come after Me," Jesus said, "he must deny himself, and take up his cross daily and follow Me" (Luke 9:23).

1. Consider this perspective: Where have you seen your own expectations or desires for a pleasant and comfortable life challenged by Jesus' call to follow Him? How did you wrestle through the situation? What was the outcome of following (or failing to follow) Him?

A Messiah by many other names. When Jesus walked on earth, He was hailed by others or referred to Himself using a variety of names. What do the following names tell you about the Messiah's relationship to God and to you?

- Rabboni (Aramaic derivative of the Hebrew "Rabbi"): Mark 10:51; John 20:16

- The Son of the Blessed One or the Son of God: Mark 14:61-62; John 20:30-31

- The Son of Man: Matthew 16:13; Mark 14:61-62; (see Daniel 7:13-14)

- The Son of David: Matthew 1:1; 9:27; 21:9; (see Isaiah 9:6-7)

- Prophet: Matthew 21:11; Luke 24:19; (see Deuteronomy 18:18-19)

- God: John 1:1-3; 20:27-29

INTERSECTIONS

Levy the power of prophecy. One untapped resource Christians can use in presenting the gospel involves showing a nonbeliever all the prophecies from the Old Testament that were fulfilled by Jesus. Using a Bible reference work, or the wisdom of a knowledgeable friend, identify one prophecy from the Old Testament regarding the Messiah's

- Lineage

- Circumstances of birth

- Nature of ministry

- Death

- Exaltation

Rather than imagining how a non-Christian friend or family member would respond to these prophecies, set up a time to discuss what you've learned with someone who would be approachable. Feel free to take your notes along, open your Bible to an Old Testament passage, and then point out the fulfillment of the promise in Jesus in the New Testament.

Let Jesus answer for Himself. There is a prevalent misconception that Jesus never claimed to be the Messiah, but that His followers began making this claim after His death. To address this misconception, it would be best to step aside and let Jesus speak for Himself.

In three consecutive chapters, John records episodes where Jesus affirmed His unique identity as the Son of God. The reaction of His listeners dispels any question about what He claimed. Read the following passages and answer the questions:

PASSAGES	WHAT DOES JESUS STATE OR IMPLY ABOUT HIS IDENTITY?	HOW DO THE PEOPLE JESUS IS SPEAKING TO RESPOND?
John 8:48-59		
John 9:13-41		
John 10:22-31		

Showing your non-Christian friends and family members Jesus' own statements about His identity will help them avoid the mistake that C. S. Lewis identified in *Mere Christianity*:

> I am trying here to prevent anyone saying the really foolish thing that people often say about Him: "I'm ready to accept Jesus as a great moral teacher, but I don't accept His claim to be God." That is the one thing we must not say. A man who was merely a man and said the sort of things Jesus said would not be a great moral teacher. He would either be a lunatic—on a level with the man who says he is a poached egg—or else he would be the Devil of Hell. You must make your choice. Either this man was, and is, the Son of God: or else a madman or something worse. You can shut Him up for a fool, you can spit at Him and kill Him as a demon; or you can fall at His feet and call Him Lord and God. But let us not come with any patronising nonsense about His being a great human teacher. He has not left that open to us. He did not intend to.[3]

Does Lewis' argument ring true to you? So many people in our day are willing to accept Jesus as a "wise teacher" and even a "revered social reformer." But the Messiah? The Son of God? That's going too far. Yet Jesus' own words leave no room for doubt as to His claim about being the one and only Messiah, sent from God as the Savior of mankind.

LAY IT TO YOUR HEART

Meditate on the following passages and commit them to memory:

- Therefore the Lord Himself will give you a sign: Behold, a virgin will be with child and bear a son, and she will call His name Immanuel. (Isaiah 7:14)
- But as for you, Bethlehem Ephrathah, too little to be among the clans of Judah, from you One will go forth for Me to be ruler

in Israel. His goings forth are from long ago, from the days of eternity. (Micah 5:2)

- Of Him all the prophets bear witness that through His name everyone who believes in Him receives forgiveness of sins. (Acts 10:43)

THE TERMS OF OUR SALVATION

THE NEW COVENANT DEFINES OUR RELATIONSHIP WITH GOD ::

Perhaps you've heard someone say, "Sure, the Bible is full of great wisdom and inspiring stories, but can a book that old really be relevant to contemporary life?"

We would do well to *question* that question before we attempt to answer it.

And we should begin by asking whether the Bible actually seems irrelevant to anyone who has read it in a sincere attempt to understand and apply it. If a person has reached a verdict of "irrelevant" without giving the Bible a fair hearing, we would have to conclude that sheer bias is at work.

Next, we should ask whether we typically measure a book's relevance on the basis of how old it is. Certainly, Nichomachus' *Introduction to Arithmetic* is as old as many books of the Bible. Do we consider the ancient principles of arithmetic irrelevant to modern astronomy or physics?

Finally, we should consider what is meant by the term irrelevant. People who lay that claim probably mean something like, "The Bible does not talk about the things that are important to me." This may well be true; however, we should probably ask the question, "Am I paying attention to things that are truly important?"

Consider a distracted driver on the highway. He is fidgeting with the radio and talking on a cell phone. He's searching for some station broadcasting the championship football game. All the while, the oil pressure is steadily dropping in his car, and the dashboard gauge is telling him about it. No one would conclude that the oil pressure gauge is irrelevant to the driver. The driver is simply too busy with other, less important matters, to pay attention to it.

So is the Bible relevant to our lives today? We have every reason to go to the Bible—and its Author—to pose this very question.

We find that the Bible reveals how man relates (and must relate!) to God. The revelation goes further than the simple assertion that God created everyone, and so we all retain some creaturely dependence or mysterious accountability to Him. These things are true, but they do not go far enough. In fact, they don't go much beyond the second chapter of the Bible.

If you read past Genesis 2, you begin to notice a pattern. God periodically interrupts the flow of human history to announce or clarify the terms by which man will have a right relationship with Him. The Scriptures call these terms "covenants," and we find that God relates to man (and vice versa) solely on the basis of them.

In essence, God has said, "This is how you and I will get along. I will be your God and you will be My people, and we will walk together along these lines. So that you do not misunderstand, I will spell things out for you."

We see the first example in the Garden of Eden, where God gave Adam and Eve certain responsibilities and certain blessings. He also bound them to one prohibition, namely that they not eat from the Tree of the Knowledge of Good and Evil lest they die. No one today relates to God on the basis of this covenant because Adam and Eve broke it.

The covenant God established with Noah when he exited from the ark is still in effect. So is the covenant God made with Abraham, when He vowed to bless all the nations through him. But what about the covenant God made with Israel at Sinai, where He gave the people His Law? Would this be an eternal covenant? Would God always relate to Israel and the rest of humanity on the basis of that agreement?

People in Jesus' day might have assumed the answer to these questions was "Yes." It appears from the gospels that few were prepared for God to alter the terms of His covenant with man in Christ.

Yet this is precisely the message that Jesus presented at the Last Supper — and the message that His followers began to proclaim after His ascension. As we listen to them teach us about the New Covenant, they point us back to the Old Testament. The message was there all along. It just couldn't be seen plainly until Christ brought it all together.

A GUIDED EXPEDITION

The inauguration of the New Covenant. As Jesus made His way to Jerusalem toward the end of His earthly ministry, His disciples assumed they would simply celebrate the Passover. They did not expect that Jesus would be arrested, tried, and summarily executed within a matter of hours. Luke 22:14-27 tells the story of Jesus' final Passover seder, which became the first Communion (or Eucharist) of the church.

1. What historical event does the Passover commemorate? See Exodus 12:23-27 for background.

2. Though you may not be familiar with the Passover seder, you can probably spot some unique, even unsettling, things Jesus said during the dinner. List a couple of them here, and comment on the effect these might have produced in Jesus' disciples.

3. Jews eat unleavened bread at Passover to remember their hurried flight from bondage in Egypt. What significance does Jesus ascribe to the bread that He breaks and passes around?

::DIFFERENT NAMES

Throughout history, Christians have called the ceremony Jesus inaugurated in Luke 22 by various names: The Lord's Supper, Communion, or the Holy Eucharist. Paul designates this ceremony the Lord's Supper in 1 Corinthians 11:20, "Therefore, when you meet together, it is not to eat the Lord's Supper." Earlier in the same letter, he had described the bread and cup as "the communion of the blood of Christ . . . the communion of the body of Christ (1 Corinthians 10:16, KJV). The term *Eucharist* is the most ancient term, and it comes from the Greek word meaning "thanksgiving." Before Jesus distributed the cup and bread, He gave thanks (1 Corinthians 11:23-24).

4. In the ritual celebration of Passover, four cups of wine are poured and passed around for all to drink. (Luke mentions only two in his brief report.) What symbol did Jesus intend His disciples to see in the wine that He poured after the meal?

5. When Jesus tipped off the disciples that one of them would betray Him to death, they fell into a discussion about who this would be. It seems their efforts to discern who was the worst among them turned effortlessly into a discussion about who was the greatest. How did Jesus turn the tables on their thinking about greatness? Also consider how His example at that meal (see John 13:5-20) and at the cross (John 19:16-30) reinforced His message.

6. Describe what kind of impact the sacrament of Communion has had on you. Also consider these questions: Is there merit in receiving Communion without reflecting on the body and blood of Jesus? What frame of mind ought to characterize someone who partakes in Communion?

The excellence of the New Covenant. More than once, Paul had to defend his own credentials as a church leader, even in the fellowships he helped to found! Those who made a show of their own authority and introduced an adulterated gospel into the church regularly attacked Paul's reputation. Thus, Paul periodically had to speak up in his own defense as he did in 2 Corinthians 3:5-18.

7. According to 2 Corinthians 3:5-6, where did Paul find the boldness to preach his gospel?

8. What contrasts does Paul draw between the nature of the Old Covenant and that of the new one in 2 Corinthians 3:5-11?

9. List the two reasons (2 Corinthians 3:7,13) Moses covered his face with a veil when he left the presence of God in the tabernacle. How does Paul contrast this with his own ministry under the New Covenant?

10. As Paul considers the response of some Jews to the gospel, he concludes that many still cannot see through the mosaic veil to perceive Christ's glory. How does Paul characterize the condition of those who reject the gospel? Describe the difference experienced by a person who turns to the Lord.

11. In Christ, the veil has been lifted. Everyone who believes in Him may behold God's glory and be transformed into Christ's likeness. What connection have you observed in your own life between beholding the Lord's glory and being made like Him?

::THE MAJOR BIBLICAL COVENANTS

There are six key covenants introduced in the Scriptures, all of them centering around a prominent figure in Israel's history. God made covenants with or through Adam (Genesis 2:16-17; Hosea 6:7), Noah (Genesis 9:8-17), Abraham (Genesis 15:1-21), Moses (Genesis 24:3-8), David (2 Samuel 7:8-16; 2 Chronicles 21:7), and Jesus (Hebrews 8:6; 9:15-16).

The efficacy of the New Covenant. The writer of Hebrews identifies an astounding implication in the Old Testament prophecies about a "new" covenant. If God was introducing into history a new means of redemptively relating to people, that must mean He was setting the old means aside. Hebrews 9:1-28 traces just how the new ministry of Christ supersedes the old ministry of sacrifices. The writer of Hebrews begins his discourse by directing our attention to a general description of the Old Testament tabernacle.

:: WHY NOT THE TEMPLE?

When the writer of Hebrews paints his comparison between the Old and New Covenants, he references the tabernacle (the sacred tent) constructed during Moses' time rather than the more enduring temple built during Solomon's. Some people account for this curiosity by supposing the treatise of Hebrews to be written after the destruction of the temple in Jerusalem AD 70. It is more probable, however, that the tabernacle's association with the Mosaic covenant made a more fit comparison with Jesus' ministry under the New Covenant. What is more, the temple's architectural grandeur and historical longevity did not alter the sacrificial ministry that had been inaugurated on Sinai when God commanded the tabernacle to be built.

12. What significant parts of the tabernacle does the writer refer to throughout this chapter?

13. Describe the kind of ministry that took place in the tabernacle. What did the ceremonies and sacrifices accomplish? (If you have no familiarity with the service at the tabernacle, Leviticus 1–8 will give you an overview.)

14. In what respects does the writer of Hebrews claim that Jesus' sacrifice was a better one than the animal sacrifices in the tabernacle?

::SEALING THE DEAL

When people enter into a contractual agreement today, they generally shake hands or sign forms. When God entered into covenants with His people in the Bible, it was generally sealed with a blood sacrifice. See, for example, the covenant with Abraham in Genesis 15 and with Israel in Exodus 24:3-8. In fact, the Hebrew expression for entering into a covenant is literally "to cut a covenant" (see Jeremiah 34:18). When God determined to cut a New Covenant with His people, He did so with a sacrifice more perfect than an unblemished sheep. He sent His own Son, whose blood not only sealed the covenant but also secured our forgiveness.

15. The writer of Hebrews says that Christ entered "heaven itself, now to appear in the presence of God for us" (9:24). In what ways does Jesus minister before God for us?

16. Hebrews 10:22-25 is one of the greatest "So what?" passages in the Bible. It gives three sensible steps that a person living under the New Covenant ought to take, each of them beginning with the phrase, "Let us . . . ." List the three steps below, and explain what it looks like for you to walk in this way.

AN OLD TESTAMENT EXCURSION

When royal officials drafted covenants in the ancient Near East, they often included provisions for what would happen if one party failed to uphold his end of the bargain. A covenant could certainly be broken, as marriage vows or business contracts are today.

But what about the covenant God entered into with Israel at Sinai? It was unthinkable that God should fail in His obligations (see Numbers 23:19). But what about Israel? So strong was the certainty that Israel would turn away from God that the Law itself revealed what would happen when they did (see Leviticus 26; Deuteronomy 28).

When Israel began to turn away from God and toward idolatry, God did not bring swift judgment on His people; instead, He forgave and overlooked many of their offenses. In the end, however, He brought His promised judgment against them for their habitual and wholehearted rejection of the covenant. Jeremiah and Ezekiel both lived during this time of judgment, as God exiled all the Jewish people from their homeland for a period of seventy years.

1. If you had lived during those days of judgment, how would these Scriptures have shaped your understanding of the status of the Old Covenant? What about your expectations of what was to come under the New Covenant?

- Jeremiah 31:27-34

- Ezekiel 16:60-63

REFLECTIONS

Hope and help from an eternal High Priest. The writer of Hebrews wrote that Jesus became for us the mediator of the New Covenant because of the power of His indestructible life. Thus, we have "a better hope, through which we draw near to God. . . . [For Jesus] is able also to save forever those who draw near to God through Him, since He always lives to make intercession for them" (Hebrews 7:19,25). In other words, we draw near to God on the basis of the hope that Jesus brought us.

1. Offer two synonyms for the word "hope" as it is being used in this passage.

2. How does your hope in Jesus influence your sense of freedom in drawing near to God? (See also Hebrews 4:14-16.)

3. Jesus is not simply the Prophet foretold in Deuteronomy 18:18-19 or the King prophesied in Psalm 2:7-12, He is also the Priest predicted in Psalm 110:4 (cited in Hebrews 7:17). What kind of ministry do you think Jesus exercises—or wants to exercise—as the Priest of your life?

God spells it out for us. When a Christian claims that God has announced the terms by which man must relate to Him in Christ —namely the New Covenant— there's a risk of sounding presumptuous. It may seem that we're boasting about having an "inside track" to God and that we know the "secret code" for maintaining a good relationship with the Almighty.

Keep in mind, however, that many Scriptures in the Old and New Testaments testify that God reveals His redemptive plan to man. He does not leave us wandering in the dark, wondering how to come into the light. God has, in fact, told His children the way to relate to Him. What God has willed to make plain, we need not pretend to be obscure.

4. What do the following passages teach you about God's desire to make His will known to man? And what do they teach you about man's ability and responsibility to proclaim this revelation to others?

- Isaiah 42:5-9

- Isaiah 46:10

- Ezekiel 33:1-9

- Amos 3:7-8

- Mark 4:21-25

- Ephesians 3:1-6

INTERSECTIONS

Coming to terms with the New Covenant. The New Covenant declares that in Christ a person may be saved from sin. However, the terms of the New Covenant are neither broad nor open to interpretation. God has set them and decreed that we may have life in Jesus if we will die to ourselves. The terms of the New Covenant amount to the terms of our surrender, and no rebel likes to surrender.

1. Describe the difficulty you have experienced in laying down your "weapons" and surrendering yourself to God on His terms.

2. Did God use any particular circumstances in your life to introduce you to His terms for your salvation? Which Scriptures, if any, helped you understand His call more clearly?

3. Under what circumstances should you present the gospel to a person by simply spelling out the terms of the New Covenant and inviting that person to respond? When might such an approach be counterproductive?

4. Describe the kind of impact your example can have on your nonbelieving friends when they see you living in the surrender, service, and hope demanded by the New Covenant.

Many paths to God. Consider the Christian belief that God relates to a person only on the basis of the New Covenant in Christ. Compare and contrast this with the popular view that there are many paths to God.

5. Do these worldviews share any hopes or doctrines in common?

6. How do the proponents of each view define the boundaries of true belief and right behavior? Describe the appeal that each might make to a "lost" person.

LAY IT TO YOUR HEART

Meditate on the following passages and commit them to memory:

- "Behold, days are coming," declares the LORD, "when I will make a new covenant with the house of Israel and with the house of Judah." (Jeremiah 31:31)
- "Behold, I am going to send My messenger, and he will clear the way before Me. And the Lord, whom you seek, will suddenly come to His temple; and the messenger of the covenant, in whom you delight, behold, He is coming," says the LORD of hosts. (Malachi 3:1)
- [Jesus] is also the mediator of a better covenant, which has been enacted on better promises. (Hebrews 8:6)

::9

THE DAWN OF A NEW DAY

AWAKENING TO THE REALITIES OF THE END OF TIME ::

The world is largely divided into two groups of people: those who grant themselves permission to read the last pages of a book out of order and those who feel an obligation to read the entire story before learning how it ends.

There is very little shared perspective between these two groups of people. Yet even those who believe the earth would spin off its axis if they read the end of a book prematurely feel a strong compulsion to do so when a good story reaches the height of suspense. In the same way, some of us have turned to the final pages of Revelation just to see how it all ends. Just to get some sense of God's genius as an author . . . and peacemaker.

For those who must know how it ends, Revelation gives sufficient detail about the end of time. For those who don't want to know the ending until the end, there is still sufficient mystery about when it all will happen!

Just look at the last sentences: "He [Jesus] who testifies to these things says, 'Yes, I am coming quickly.' Amen. Come, Lord Jesus. The grace of the Lord Jesus be with all. Amen" (Revelation 22:20-21).

You cannot escape the certainty about Jesus' Second Coming. Two "amens" in as many sentences. Even Jesus Himself testifies to the fact of His return. The present era will draw to a close when Jesus steps back onto the stage of human history.

But when will He return? Who can fail to feel the indeterminacy about that word "quickly"? We've been waiting now for two thousand years! But who can say what "quickly" means to the One who created time itself?

We are certain that Jesus will come back and uncertain about when it will happen. God has gratified our curiosity to know how the story will end but left us with the dramatic tension of when it will all be resolved. The Great Author has given us a book that everyone can be happy with.

Or has He? It is sobering to consider just how grave the biblical portrait of the Day of the Lord is. The words of the prophet Amos come to mind: "Alas, you who are longing for the day of the LORD, for what purpose will the day of the LORD be to you? It will be darkness and not light" (Amos 5:18). The people in Amos' time rightly understood that the Day of the Lord was a day of wrath against God's enemies and salvation for His children. However, they made the mistake of assuming that all Gentiles were His enemies and all Jews His friends.

What Amos made plain, the New Testament writers made even more clear: "There will be tribulation and distress for every soul of man who does evil, of the Jew first and also of the Greek, but glory and honor and peace to everyone who does good, to the Jew first and also to the Greek" (Romans 2:9-10).

On the Day of Judgment, there will be no discrimination. Instead, there will be a division between those who have loved God and honored His Son and those who have not. The future should not seem rosy to people who have rejected God's revelation, His Scriptures, and His Son.

If it does, they should take off the rose-colored glasses.

But how should you respond to the teachings about the final days? How does the prospect of the imminent return of Jesus rest in your soul? For one last time in this study, let's allow Scripture to show us the way.

A GUIDED EXPEDITION

Be watchful! Jesus told His disciples to prepare for the time when the temple in Jerusalem would be destroyed. They seized upon this comment to ask Him about the signs that would precede His coming and about the end of the age. Matthew 24:24-51 records Jesus' response to this question.

1. Describe the confusion that Jesus predicts near the end of the age (verses 24-26).

:: THE FATE OF THE TEMPLE

Jesus' teachings about the destruction of the temple might have confused his original audience. Most Jews believed along with the Rabbis that the advent of the Messiah would spell the cessation of ministry in the temple, but not its destruction. As it happened, Jesus came and went, while the ministry of the temple continued until AD 70. At that time, Jerusalem fell to the Roman general, Titus, who sacked the city and razed the temple. It has never been rebuilt. On the site of the ancient temple today stands a Muslim shrine called the Dome of the Rock.

2. Jesus says that no one will have room for doubt when He comes again (verses 27-31). What portents will appear when Jesus returns?

3. How did Jesus advise us to live and act in light of His Second Coming (verses 12-14,24,26)?

4. What lesson does Jesus want His disciples to learn from the fig tree? And what lesson does He want to impart through the comparison to the days of Moses?

:: WAS JESUS MISLED?

Many people have been mystified by Jesus' prediction that "this generation will not pass away until all these things take place" (Matthew 24:34). Certainly, everyone in Jesus' generation passed away prior to His Second Coming. Was Jesus misled? No. Instead, we should read this passage in the larger context of Matthew 24 "as a highly symbolic description of the theological significance of the coming destruction of the temple and its consequences."[1] We must bear in mind that Jesus had been asked to comment on the time when the temple would be destroyed *and* the time when he would come again at the end of the age (see Matthew 24:1-3).

5. Because Jesus Himself did not know the hour when He would return, He assures us that we won't either. He does, however, give us instructions about how we, as servants, should live in light of our Master's return (verses 42-51). Consider these questions and summarize your thoughts: What kind of servant does Jesus commend? What kind does He condemn? Describe the thought processes of a servant who wakes up each morning in readiness for the Master's return.

Be encouraged! The great hope we gain in the gospel is that after death we will live again in God's presence because Christ was raised from the dead. This sure hope was understood imperfectly in the first-century church of Thessalonica. They were troubled that friends from their congregation had passed away before the second advent of Jesus. Paul penned the words in 1 Thessalonians 4:13–5:11 to address their confusion. In so doing, he taught us not only how to think about death but how to think ahead to the Day of the Lord.

6. What reason do we have for expecting that those who have died in Christ will live again?

7. Describe what will actually happen to believers—both "awake" and "asleep"—at the Second Coming.

8. Poet T. S. Eliot brought "The Hollow Men" to a close by describing how the empty men of his era envisioned the end of the world. The poem ends with these famous lines:

> *This is the way the world ends.*
> *This is the way the world ends.*
> *This is the way the world ends.*
> *Not with a bang, but a whimper.*[2]

How do you suppose Paul would respond to the expectations of the "hollow men"? What phrases did he use to describe the way Jesus' return would be heralded?

:: HE CAME IN LIKE A LAMB

Jesus came to earth the first time as a small child and suffered for our sins "like a lamb that is led to slaughter, and like a sheep that is silent before its shearers" (Isaiah 53:7). No one should expect to meet Him this way again. When Paul says that "The Lord Himself will descend from heaven with a shout, with the voice of the archangel, and with the trumpet of God" (1 Thessalonians 4:16), he is calling on the imagery of a Roman military conqueror in regal procession after victory. Jesus came first in meekness. He will come finally in might and majesty.

9. Paul borrowed an image from Jesus (see Matthew 24:43) when he said, "The day of the Lord will come just like a thief in the night" (1 Thessalonians 5:2). How does Paul portray the readiness of those who do not know Jesus? What about Christians who know He is coming again?

10. How does Paul advise Christians to relate to one another in light of the Second Coming of Christ (1 Thessalonians 5:11)?

Be expectant! Few things are more difficult than walking into an unfamiliar environment with no idea of what to expect. How gracious it is that God has shaped our expectations about what to anticipate in the lead-up to the Day of the Lord! Thanks to passages like 2 Peter 3:1-15, we can orient our expectations around the truth.

11. How do verses 3-9 shape your anticipation about how much time will pass before the Day of the Lord arrives?

12. As one year gives way to the next, mockers arise to scoff at the prospect of Jesus' Second Coming. So much time has elapsed since Jesus' resurrection that the Second Coming is a difficult doctrine for many Christians to hold. How much more so a nonbeliever! What biblical perspective does Peter claim such mockers lack (verse 7)?

::NO SENSE OF HISTORY

Within thirty years of Jesus' resurrection, Peter could already anticipate the skeptical question, "Where is the promise of His coming?" (2 Peter 3:4). From whatever quarter this question arises, it betrays a short-sighted vision of history. From the Fall to the revelation of the Law, around 1,500 years passed. From the giving of the Law to the incarnation of Christ, another 2,000 years passed. Who will fault God for His timing if He adds another 500 years and sends His Son to Earth for the second time after 2,500 more years of human history have elapsed?

13. Describe your understanding of what the last days will look like, according to 2 Peter 3:1-15. What will happen to the people who are on earth?

14. Why does God delay bringing about the end of days (verse 9)?

15. With the Day of the Lord held firmly in view, "what sort of people ought [we] to be" (verse 11)?

AN OLD TESTAMENT EXCURSION

When Jesus taught about the Day of the Lord, He told His disciples about the unmistakable cosmic disruption that would accompany it. It seems realistic to see some change in the skies when the new heavens and earth displace the old (Revelation 21:1).

Even so, the cosmic shakeup is not exactly a natural phenomenon. It is a prophetic symbol, almost a rhetorical device that Jesus drew on. Every prophet of the Old Testament connected divine judgment with heavenly chaos. God's wrath against the wicked is written in the stars, you might say. It is worth exploring this symbol for yourself so that when you read about it in the New Testament, you will sense the significance with the rest of the revelation.

1. Examine each of the following Old Testament texts and answer these questions: Who is the prophecy directed against? What divine judgment do the heavens declare?

THE PROPHET AND PASSAGE	WHO IS THE PROPHECY DIRECTED AGAINST?	WHAT DIVINE JUDGMENTS DO THE HEAVENS DECLARE?
Isaiah 13:6-16		
Jeremiah 4:23-28		
Ezekiel 32:2-8		
Joel 3:9-17		
Amos 8:7-10		
Zephaniah 1:14-18		

REFLECTIONS

Planning for the Day of the Lord. As we have observed, the Day of the Lord is a day of judgment and a day of salvation. Jesus confirms this point in Matthew 24:42-51 when He declares that His return will be like a Master returning to His own household. The servant who is watching for Him and tending to His affairs will find grace and gladness at His coming. The one who has ignored the Master's interests and served his own will meet with condemnation.

1. How do you respond to this double-sided promise of salvation and judgment on the Day of the Lord? Write down two or three things that you are doing or could do to remain alert and watchful for the coming of Jesus.

2. Over what affairs has Jesus put you in charge until He comes back?

3. Do you live alongside friends or family members who you suspect will meet with judgment on the Day of the Lord? How might you turn your concern for their welfare into practical action and prayers for their salvation?

The Day in a different light. The Day of the Lord is referred to in various ways in the Bible and the church. Reflecting on these various descriptions will deepen your appreciation of the significance of that Day. How do the following designations reveal some new facet of the "great and awesome Day of the Lord" (Joel 2:31)?

- Judgment Day (Matthew 10:15; Acts 17:31; 1 John 4:17)

- The Second Coming (Acts 1:11; Hebrews 9:28)

- The End Times (Matthew 24:12-14; 1 Peter 4:7)

INTERSECTIONS

Reckoning the days. Many people actively ignore the fact that their life will someday come to an end. How much less does the average person think about the end of the world! It's not that people have no thoughts on the subject; it simply doesn't come up in day-to-day conversation.

Yet the Bible calls this kind of neglect to account: "LORD, make me to know my end and what is the extent of my days," King David prays. "Let me know how transient I am. Behold, You have made my days as handbreadths, and my lifetime as nothing in Your sight; surely every man at his best is a mere breath" (Psalm 39:4-5).

Introduce the subject of the end of the world to a few non-Christian friends just to find out what they think. Do they think it matters? Do they care? If so, how do they view it? Do they imagine the world will go on forever or that it will wind down to a final point? If a final point, will it wind down because of natural causes, human stupidity, or divine intervention? Will it end with a "bang" or with a "whimper," as T. S. Eliot put it?

You could approach a non-Christian friend with words like these, "I'd like to get your thoughts on the possibility that this world will not last forever. I've been doing a study on what the Bible teaches about it." Remember, you are soliciting information, not offering it. Do not feel compelled to correct any response the person gives. Of course, you should be prepared to field questions, including what you have learned from the Bible about the end of the world.

The sweet here and now. People in our society place a lot of faith in the progress of technology and medicine, so much so that they are skeptical of any belief system that leads them away from a head-on engagement with the world's problems. Some folks say, "We want none of that 'pie in the sky' stuff. We need a religion that works in this world, not one that leaves us pining away for another one."

Yet how might a disregard for the afterlife actually hinder progress in this world? How might it distract a person from things that are important in his or her own soul? Suggest two or three ways that Christian confidence in the Day of the Lord has motivated a commitment to change the world today.

LAY IT TO YOUR HEART

Meditate on the following passages and commit them to memory:

- Therefore be on the alert, for you do not know which day your Lord is coming. (Matthew 24:42)
- Christ also, having been offered once to bear the sins of many, will appear a second time for salvation without reference to sin, to those who eagerly await Him. (Hebrews 9:28)
- The night is almost gone, and the day is near. Therefore let us lay aside the deeds of darkness and put on the armor of light. (Romans 13:12)

NOTES

CHAPTER ONE: A FIRM FOUNDATION

1. Mortimer Adler, ed., *The Great Books of the Western World: Lucretius*, vol. 12, "On the Nature of Things," II, 644 (University of Chicago Press, 1956), 23.

2. Adler, ed., *The Great Books of the Western World: Marcus Aurelius*, vol. 12, "Meditations," III, 7, 261.

3. Cited in Abraham Cohen, *Everyman's Talmud: The Major Teachings of the Rabbinic Sages* (New York: Schocken Books, 1995), 3.

4. C. S. Lewis, *God in the Dock*, ed. Walter Hooper (Grand Rapids, Mich.: Eerdmans, 2000), 41.

5. G. K. Chesterton. *The Everlasting Man* (San Francisco: Ignatius Press, 1993), 23.

6. Adler, ed., *The Great Books of the Western World: Pascal*, vol. 33, *Penseés, IV,* 218.

CHAPTER TWO: A POLLUTED SOURCE

1. G. K. Chesterton, *The Everlasting Man* (San Francisco: Ignatius, 1993), 53.
2. John MacArthur, *The MacArthur Study Bible*, notes to Romans 8:2 (Nashville, TN: Word, 1997), 1706.
3. Cited in Eusebius, *Ecclesiastical History*, II, 23 (Peabody, MA: Hendrickson Publishers, 1998), 59–60.
4. C. S. Lewis, *Surprised by Joy, The Beloved Works of C. S. Lewis* (Grand Rapids, MI: Family Christian Press, 1998), 57.

CHAPTER THREE: AN OPEN INVITATION

1. Spiros Zodhiates *The Complete Word Study Dictionary: New Testament.* Entry 3466: "Musterion" (Chattanooga, TN: AMG International, 1993), 1000.
2. Francis Thompson, *The Works of Francis Thompson: Poems, Volume II* (London: Burns, Oates, & Washbourne, 1913), 225.

CHAPTER FOUR: FREE AT LAST

1. Jerry Bridges, *The Discipline of Grace* (Colorado Springs, CO: NavPress, 1994), 76.
2. Henry David Thoreau, *Walden, or Life in the Woods* in Baym, et al., *The Norton Antology of American Literature*, third edition, vol. 1 (New York: W. W. Norton and Company, 1989), 1652.

CHAPTER FIVE: RIGHTEOUSNESS WITHIN REACH

1. Mortimer Adler, ed., *The Great Books of the Western World: Plutarch*, vol. 14, "Lycurgus" (University of Chicago Press, 1956), 47.
2. See Benjamin Blech, *Understanding Judaism: The Basics of Deed and Creed* (Lanham, MD: Jason Aronson, 1991), 175-181. Also see Abraham Cohen, *Everyman's Talmud: The Major Teachings of the Rabbinic Sages* (New York: Schocken Books, 1995), 61–66.

CHAPTER SEVEN: A MAN CALLED MESSIAH

1. Mortimer Adler, ed., *The Great Books of the Western World: Pascal,* vol. 33, *Pensées,* XI, 710 (Chicago: University of Chicago Press, 1956), 303.

2. Adler, *The Great Books of the Western World: Pascal,* XI, 706, 303–306.

3. C. S. Lewis, *Mere Christianity* (New York: Collier Books, 1960), 55-56.

CHAPTER NINE: THE DAWN OF A NEW DAY

1. R. T. France, *The Gospel According to Matthew: An Introduction and Commentary* (Grand Rapids, MI: Intervarsity Press, 1986), 343-346.

2. T. S. Eliot, "The Hollow Men" in *The Complete Poems and Plays 1909-1950* (New York: Harcourt Brace Jovanovich, 1952), 59.

ABOUT THE AUTHOR

NORMAN HUBBARD, a native of South Carolina, serves as the campus director for The Navigators at the University of Illinois at Urbana-Champaign. He graduated from Auburn University with an MA in English (applied linguistics). Norman and his wife, Katie, have three children in elementary school.

DIG INTO GOD'S WORD WITH THESE GREAT BIBLE STUDIES.

Left of Matthew
Norman Hubbard
978-1-60006-052-6   1-60006-052-8

This companion study to *Right of Malachi* explores the unifying stories and themes woven throughout Scripture, encouraging readers to actively engage the text and move beyond simple summaries.

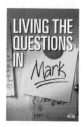

Living the Questions in Mark
The Navigators
978-1-57683-860-0   1-57683-860-9

Using this ten-week study, readers and small groups can grapple with some of the provocative questions Jesus posed to his followers in the gospel of Mark, enabling them to embrace life's uncertainties and strengthen their faith.

Living the Questions in Luke
The Navigators
978-1-57683-861-7   1-57683-861-7

This thought-provoking study of the gospel of Luke will help readers wrestle personally with the often-unsettling questions Jesus asked. Includes text from *The Message*, along with real-life anecdotes and excerpts from literature, pop culture, and current events.